ACCEPTANCE

*Loosing
the Webs of
Personal
Insecurity*

ACCEPTANCE

Loosing the Webs of Personal Insecurity

DON BAKER

MULTNOMAH · PRESS

Portland, Oregon 97266

Unless otherwise indicated, all Scripture references are from the New American Standard Bible, © The Lockman Foundation 1960, 1962, 1963, 1968, 1971, 1972, 1973, 1975, 1977. Used by permission.

Cover design by Steve Eames
Edited by Larry R. Libby

ACCEPTANCE
© 1985 by Don Baker
Published by Multnomah Press
Portland, Oregon 97266

Printed in the United States of America

Library of Congress Cataloging in Publication Data

Baker, Don.
    Acceptance.

    1. Meditations.   2. Baker, Don.   I. Title.
    BV4832.2.B259   1984   242   84-27246
    ISBN 0-88070-079-3

85 86 87 88 89 90 91 – 10 9 8 7 6 5 4 3 2 1

TO MARTHA
My wife, who inspired
the writing of this book, and
who has accepted me.

Contents

_____

"I am still trying to
gain that complete
freedom that has
eluded me for so long."

_____

Chapter One

The Cocoon

I received a most unusual gift the other day—small, boxed, and beautifully wrapped. I opened it with excitement, carefully removing ribbon, wrapping, and finally lifting the lid.

What was this? Some sort of joke?

The box contained a small twig of wood about six inches in length. Attached to the twig was the ugliest little "whatever" I think I have ever seen. At first glance it appeared to be the color and texture of a long-since dead mouse. I laughed—nervously—all the time realizing that my friend was not sharing my humor.

I touched it—lightly—smelled it, examined it, and finally asked, "What in the world is it?"

"Don't you know?" my friend asked. "It's something you mention often. You even use it to illustrate the Christian life. It's a *cocoon*. It's the cocoon of a beautiful, multi-colored, giant silk moth. I bought it the other day, thinking you might like to watch the transformation of something ugly into something very beautiful.

"In just a few weeks, without any noticeable outward

change, the living organism in that ugly little brown cocoon will free itself and emerge into—well, you'll see."

I was intrigued. After my friend left, I placed the cocoon in a little net cage near the window and began to watch.

Weeks have passed. There has been no noticeable change—no movement of any kind. It's still brown, ugly, and apparently lifeless. And yet, inside that hideous little shell is a living thing—a small caterpillar—actively engaged in the struggling process of gaining its freedom and becoming beautiful.

While still in the larval state, that little living thing spun a web around itself—an endless web of silk and sand and dirt. Finally, when completely hidden in a prison of its own making, it then began the long, slow, painful process of gaining its freedom.

I've read of this metamorphosis, this change from imprisoned caterpillar to colorful butterfly, many times, but I've never watched it. I never realized just how ugly a cocoon could really be. I didn't know it took so long. I'd never heard just how hard that emerging creature would be forced to struggle—and without any outside help. In fact, assistance of any kind would cause it to die. Breaking free of that cocoon is something that must be done. It must be done with great pain, and it must be done all alone.

As I have daily examined my woolly little friend in its ugly brown cocoon, bound so tightly in that web, I have come to realize that I'm not only watching the emergence of a butterfly, I'm watching something far more profound and frighteningly personal. I'm actually watching humanity engaged in its constant struggle to free itself of its webs, its hang-ups, its bindings, its prisons. Webs of its own making—webs spun by others—webs that have bound so tightly and so thoroughly that the real occupant in that little house has become completely obscured to the outside world.

I'm watching myself, hidden by external wrappings, imprisoned by internal fears, bound by the trappings of society and confined by the prejudices of people and even some distorted truths of Christianity. I am still trying to gain that complete freedom that has eluded me for so long.

I am watching my own determined struggle to be free of all of the suffocating webs that still hide me from myself and from those who would wish to love me.

―――――――――――

"It seems, at times, that
life's greatest struggle
may not be that of
loving, but rather
that of accepting love."

―――――――――――

Chapter Two

In Hiding

I really don't know when I went into hiding. I do know that at some time and for some reason not completely known to me, I began spinning a web—a web consisting of the strangest notions—neurotic little notions of

inferiority
inadequacy
guilt
rejection
unworthiness
insecurity
tentativeness
ambivalence—

notions that caused me to be guarded and withdrawn, to feel unloving and unloved.

It's awfully hard for me to receive love. That admission would be difficult if I didn't believe that so many others, like myself, have the same problem. I'm one of a vast army of internally frightened and lonely people who have built an impenetrable web about themselves. This web makes it impossible for others to move in close and to love and to affirm and to assure and to accept.

At the same time, I genuinely doubt that there are many people who are more loved than I. God loves me, my family loves me, my church loves me, my friends love me, my dog loves me. Thousands of friends each year send affirming messages of love. Hardly a day goes by without a love note from someone who has been touched by my ministry.

My internal responses to such gestures of love are often baffling. Outwardly, I appear grateful, pleased, secure, and believing. Inwardly, I question motives, suspect manipulation, doubt another's integrity, or more commonly, hope that those who say they love me will never discover how truly unworthy I am of their love.

It seems at times that life's greatest struggle may not be that of loving, but rather that of accepting love. Somewhere in life I, along with others, have picked up the mistaken notion that love and acceptance are marketable commodities, to be dispensed only to purchase something felt to be of value. People who feel no worth or value within themselves could never expect to enjoy unqualified love or acceptance.

I sat with two friends recently discussing "acceptance." Both are happily married Christians, students of the Scriptures, and outwardly secure and happy. I asked them, "Do you feel accepted by God?" They both answered, "Certainly we have been accepted by God. Ephesians 1:6 says that part of the total experience of becoming a Christian means that we have been 'accepted in the beloved'" (KJV). "That's not what I asked," I said. "Do you *feel* accepted by God?" They both thought for a moment and answered, "No." One went on to say, "I don't even feel forgiven by God—I believe I am, but I don't feel like it."

I then asked, "Do you feel accepted by your wives?" Again there was a pause, and both answered, "No, not completely."

"I don't even feel accepted by myself," one of them offered. Finally, with hesitancy, we all agreed to feeling exactly the same way.

As I walked away from that conversation, I thought to myself, "Where did all those suffocating webs come from that make it so difficult for us to feel comfortable with ourselves? Why is it so impossible to feel comfortable with God? Why do we struggle so to feel comfortable with others?" And really, that's all acceptance is and that's all acceptance says—it's just the experience of being totally comfortable with others.

I have no difficulty explaining those feelings of discomfort in the lives of those who have never experienced the love and forgiveness of God. My problem is that so many of my Christian friends, including myself, seem to still be imprisoned in that stifling little cocoon, living only partial lives and longing for that elusive freedom that seems so distant—so impossible.

"My difficulty in accepting myself has made it extremely hard to accept others."

Chapter Three

Spinning the Webs

I have always had difficulty accepting myself.

I think I must have begun spinning my own web when I first began hearing ugly statements about myself—statements that were meant to be harmless, yet have remained ingrained in my memory. Statements like:

"You sure do have a big nose."

"You're so fat I can't even see your collar."

"Your legs are awfully short."

"Why are your hands so stubby?"

"You have more freckles than anyone I've ever seen."

"Did you know you have a slight lisp?"

"Boy, you've got a lot of moles on your back."

"You're so barrel-chested you should wear a bra."

"Why do you hold your mouth like that?"

"Can't you find clothes that fit you?"

"I wish you weren't so sensitive."

"Man, you're stupid."

"And you call yourself a Christian?"

None of these many statements was designed to be destructive, and had I been less sensitive, none of them would probably have even been remembered. But they were spoken, and I am sensitive, and they are remembered. When I combine them with the many other negative comments I have picked up through the years, they seem to paint a picture of an ugly self that wants to go into permanent hiding.

Now, please don't misunderstand me—not all the things that have been said to me or about me are negative. I suppose for each negative comment I have received, I've heard a thousand heart-warming, gracious, generous, loving compliments.

For some strange reason, though, my memory seems to be warped in the direction of the negative—it dwells on the negative—it remembers the negative—it believes the negative, and as it does, it sees an image of self that is negative and totally unacceptable.

When I first began hearing God describe me in the Scriptures, again all I heard was the negative. He said:

> I am filled with all
> > unrighteousness,
> > > wickedness,
> > > > greed, and
> > > > > malice.
> I am full of
> > envy,
> > > murder,
> > > > strife, and
> > > > > deceit.
> I am a gossip,
> > a slanderer.
> I hate God.
> I am insolent,
> > arrogant,
> > > boastful.
> I actually invent evil.
> I am disobedient to my parents.

I am without understanding,
        untrustworthy,
            unloving, and
                unmerciful.

And not only am I guilty of such things, I actually encourage others to do the same.[1]

A biblical passage like that is anything but complimentary. It certainly did very little for my self-image except to cause me to start spinning webs—fast. If that's the real me—I wasn't quite sure how God found it out—I was determined that it must be hid at all costs.

There was nothing in that list of characteristics that was acceptable to me or to anyone else.

How could I accept myself—be comfortable with myself—if that was the real me?

I have not only had difficulty accepting myself, I have also had a problem accepting God, and even greater problems feeling accepted by him.

My first impressions of God were those of some sort of cosmic judge, just waiting to bang down the gavel of his cosmic justice whenever my performance failed to measure up to his heavenly standards.

Like most Christians my age, and even younger, I was weaned on little songs like:

Be careful, little eyes, what you see,
Be careful, little eyes, what you see,
For the Father up above
Is looking down in love, so
Be careful, little eyes, what you see.

Again, what could have been a very positive, reassuring message of hope—a graphic word-picture set to music that described an ever-present, watchful, attendant, loving God—spoke just the opposite to me.

The little song spoke warnings, not only to my eyes but also to my lips, my ears, my hands, even my feet, until God took on the appearance of some sort of "Big Brother" in the sky, spying on my every move, just waiting to pounce on me whenever I did or said something that displeased him.

I can remember, years after I had received Christ, sitting in church through long, intense, persuasive invitations to "sinners to come to Christ," feeling that the preacher was talking directly to me.

Why couldn't I feel the love and forgiveness of God even though I had already accepted it?

I was afraid of God. I tried to hide from him—knowing all the time it was impossible, but nevertheless trying anyway.

> God's promises seemed to always have impossible strings attached.
> God's invitations seemed always to be selective and exclude me.
> God's love seemed always to be conditional, and I never quite measured up.
> God's presence seemed always to be elusive, unattainable and beyond reach.

Was my early theological training unbalanced?

Words like *grace, love, forgiveness,* and *acceptance* were either seldom mentioned or I failed to hear them.

But words like *law, fear, shame,* and *rejection* . . . those were the terms that sifted through my hearing into my uneasy heart.

It seems that most of my early training consisted of "Thou shalt not's." I felt imprisoned by a system ingeniously designed to create constant feelings of fear and bondage.

I can remember at age nine standing by the front door of my church one Sunday morning, waiting until everyone had finally shaken my pastor's hand and then walking over to him and fearfully asking his permission to go roller-skating. Permission was denied.

A friend of mine went swimming one Sunday—dived into shallow water and fractured his neck. My first reaction was, "He should have known better than to go swimming on Sunday."

My father repaired a broken padlock one Sunday following church. The family later went for a drive. Upon returning home we were involved in an accident. Dad's first words were, "I knew I shouldn't have worked on that lock today."

Whenever I spent any time reflecting on myself, all I could see was an overweight, stoop-shouldered, freckled-faced kid whose mind always wanted to drift off into a world of happy, exciting, adventurous fantasy because the real world and the real me always looked and felt so grim.

The fact that my body, with its blemishes and imperfections, was never counterbalanced with the dynamic and freeing truth that God made me just as I am and had a divine reason for shaping every part of my being just as he did, was never brought to my attention.

I remember the first time I realized just how much divine involvement there had been in the process of my birth. I read Psalm 139:13-16 over and over again. I searched its every meaning in the various translations that were available. And something wonderful happened. At that very moment I stopped praying for someone to invent Porcelana and began thanking God for every single freckle on my body.

The fact that I was totally depraved, unrighteous and unholy, was never counterbalanced with the awesome truth that I was fearfully and wonderfully made, in the very image of Almighty God, presently as precious to God as his own dear Son and ultimately destined to be just like Jesus.

People never told me how truly wonderful I really was in God's eyes—or if they did, the contrary voices were so loud I couldn't hear them.

At age twelve, I was unexpectedly called into the principal's office. I was terrified. I was certain that doomsday had arrived. I didn't know why, but then who needed a reason?

Miss Plank was the most frightening principal I can recall. She was short, grossly fat, and was never known to smile. I never saw her without a heavy twelve-inch ruler in her hand and often heard the heavy "smack" as that piece of wood landed on unsuspecting flesh.

I crept into her office, crouched down on the bench in front of her desk, and looked at that forbidding creature as she continued to pore over the papers on her desk.

After what seemed to be an interminable period of time, she looked up, trained her eyes on me, looked deep into my naked soul, and said, "Donald Baker?"

I heard a squeaky "Yes, Miss Plank," in response.

"I was just looking over your records," she said in a deep and threatening voice, "and I noticed that today is your birthday. Today is my birthday, too," she said, "and I thought it would be nice if we could just wish each other a 'Happy Birthday!'"

With that she lumbered from behind her desk, enveloped me with her mammoth arms, and then pushed me out her door to go back to class.

Why was I so frightened?

Why was I so stunned?

Why do tears come to my eyes even now when I recall that memorable moment?

Who is the culprit responsible for making me feel so uncomfortable with myself and so clumsy around others?

Could it be that someone neglected to tell me the whole truth—or was it that my mind was just unable to comprehend it?

Half-truths, untruths, or subtle innuendos, whispered from without and within, made me feel not only uncomfortable with myself, but uncomfortable with my God.

To accept myself as I truly am and to accept my heavenly Father as he truly is and then to *feel* accepted by myself and to *feel* accepted by my Father has come with difficulty—and oftentimes with great pain.

My reluctance to accept myself has made accepting others an uphill struggle. David Seamands has said, "Some of the most powerful weapons in Satan's arsenal are psychological," and, "The most powerful psychological weapon that Satan uses against us is low self-esteem."[2]

This low self-esteem, or inability to feel comfortable with myself, makes me uncomfortable with others. My cocoon not only isolates me, but it also distorts the images of others until I begin seeing them in the same way I view myself.

Some of the hardest people to live with in all the world are the people who don't like themselves. No one knows this better than I. I have worked with people most of my life. Much of this time was spent while struggling with a strong dislike for myself. Someone asked me once, "Why are you so angry?" I never was able to tell him until I later realized that my anger was self-directed. I was angry because I could not be what I wanted to be or feel toward myself as I wanted to feel. I didn't like myself—I didn't accept myself—I was terribly uncomfortable with *me*. Too often this anger erupted and spilled over on unsuspecting victims such as wife or children or friends who never fully understood the cause of my wrath.

I have viewed others as hostile, frightening, suspicious, or deceitful. I have viewed their differences as threatening. I often developed an authoritarian and rigid stance toward many, simply as a defense mechanism that allowed me to feel freedom from questions or complaints. At times my pulpit was regarded as the impenetrable wall from which I could fire my verbal volleys with impunity. No one dared argue publicly with the preacher.

My view of myself colored my view of others, and the worst accusation I could think of—but never stated—was that another person was just as phony and evil as I.

I must admit to bigotry, to intolerance, even to chauvinism, not because I was trained in such thinking, but because my inability to accept myself made it impossible to accept others.

Someone has said the kingdom of God is a kingdom of right relationships. Christ came to make things right, not only between ourselves, but within ourselves.

An inability to accept myself made it impossible to feel comfortable with others—and the word *others* includes all the "others" who inhabit my total world. That includes God. That includes individuals. That includes a whole world that is at times outright hostile toward me.

To feel comfortable in and with this world has also posed some real problems for me. I am told not to love the world, yet God did. I am told not to be like it, yet not to withdraw from it. I am told not to seek its acclaim, yet to seek its approval. I am expected to experience its hatred, yet never to run away or retaliate.

Right relationships include all of the above—the ability to feel comfortable with myself, comfortable with my God, comfortable with others, and even comfortable with this world in which I live.

That's the meaning of the word "acceptance"—to feel comfortable with another. It's somewhat like the emerging life of a beautiful and gigantic silk-moth that has painfully freed itself from its isolation, to fly with freedom and to light gracefully with admired beauty wherever it wishes to go. It moves from one sphere of its world to another with beauty and with grace and with ease—to be admired by all.

But, you may ask, who could ever live a life like that?

Chapter 3, Notes

1. Romans 1:29-32
2. David A. Seamands, *Healing for Damaged Emotions* (Wheaton, Ill.: Victor Books, 1981), pp. 18-49.

———————————

"Jesus was the most
perfect and intriguing
example of
psychological balance
that ever lived."

———————————

Chapter Four

The Model

JESUS DID!

Jesus was the most perfect and intriguing example of psychological balance that ever lived. Whenever I read the gospels, I never cease to be impressed with his complete comfort with himself and others—never a hint of feeling threatened internally or externally.

One of the greater miracles in the earthly life of the God-man—a miracle seldom, if ever, mentioned—was the unbelievable manner in which he adapted to his new environment.

Jesus was a good candidate for a mammoth culture shock. No one has crossed cultures as he did. Coming from heaven to earth was the farthest distance physically, socially, spiritually, and psychologically that anyone could ever travel. The contrasts were unimaginable, and yet he accepted his displacement, along with his new and vastly different role, with incredible ease.

Jesus was demoted as no other being in all of history. He was lowered in rank, forced to give up his prestigious position, relinquish his wealth, change his name, even limit his energies. Yet he always appeared to be at peace with himself, his Father, his people, and even with a frighteningly hostile world.

If there was ever one who had reason to go into hiding, if there was ever an individual who could have felt justified in spinning an endless web about himself, it was Jesus. He had good reason to display all those neurotic little notions I have often struggled with, and yet there was never a moment that he even suggested a hint of such feelings.

> He came as a servant, yet never displayed inferiority.
>
> He limited his own powers, yet never suggested inadequacy.
>
> He was sent down from heaven, yet never complained of rejection.
>
> He disrobed himself of all his majesty, yet never appeared unworthy.
>
> He owned no property and possessed no home, yet never complained of feeling insecure.
>
> His days, from the very beginning, were numbered, yet he never felt tentative.
>
> He placed himself completely at the mercy of man, yet knew every moment exactly what was happening.
>
> He possessed infinite wisdom, yet was able to be completely comfortable chatting with the world's most ignorant.
>
> He was supremely holy, yet he could comfortably sit with the world's great sinners.
>
> He was Jewish, yet he had no difficulty crossing racial barriers to talk with a Samaritan.
>
> He was a man, yet he was comfortable any time and at all times with God.
>
> He was the world's Savior, yet he could move with ease even in the presence of hostile threats of murder.

Jesus accepted himself. He knew who he was and why he was here. He could accept compliments or insults without clumsy responses.

On the occasion of his baptism, his Father made a dramatic, if not somewhat embarrassing public announcement about his Son. He spoke from the heavens for all to hear that Jesus was very special to him. "Beloved" was the word he used. He even stated that his was the perfect Son and that he was truly delighted in him. That sort of parental exclamation of pride is often met with embarrassment. And yet Jesus let his Father brag about him without blushing or even responding. He knew the truth about himself, accepted it, and was totally comfortable with the facts as they stood.

Whenever he was accused of evil, even the worst of all sins, blasphemy, he met the challenge with a simple request: "Prove it. Search as hard and long as you like," he would say, "but prove it."

He even stated that Satan could find no fault in him.

Jesus never went into hiding. He never spun a web around himself or withdrew into his cocoon. His was a totally transparent life.

When asked where he lived, he gave no evasive answer. He didn't even hand out business cards with a printed address. He said simply, "Come and see." Nothing to hide, nothing to fear.

When our daughter, Kathy, was small, the first place she would always take her friends would be her bedroom. That bedroom was not only where she slept, it was a representation of herself. The most intimate declarations she could make about her person were in that one little room. All of her interests, likes, and dislikes were on display for anyone who was interested to see. That act was always the ultimate in childlike transparency.

Jesus did the same. "Come and see," he said. He didn't even run ahead to tidy things up.

For three and a half years he peeled off layer after layer of divine mystery and exposed his being to any who really wished to know him.

He hid nothing.
He knew himself.
He accepted himself.
Jesus was totally comfortable with himself.

He was also comfortable with God.

He could speak of him in the most lofty terms with total knowledge.
He could also speak of him in the most intimate language with absolute comfort.
He had no fear of God.
He experienced no separation from God.
He could spontaneously pray in public without any exaggerated preparations.
He could move into seclusion and begin talking to his Father with no feelings of guilt or requests for forgiveness.
He knew his Father always heard him.
He fully expected his Father to give him whatever he requested.
He understood his Father's heart.
He knew his Father's purpose.
He recognized his Father's wisdom.
He trusted his Father's power.
He expected his Father's full approval.
He looked forward to his Father's presence.
He even knew, and declared publicly, the fact that there was an extraordinary and quite intimate union between himself and his Father.
Jesus was totally comfortable with God.

Jesus was comfortable with people.

He accepted people.
He accepted them right where they were and for what they were.
He knew why he was with them.
He knew their need of him.
He even knew why they did what they did.

He was equally at home with—
  a scoundrel like Zacchaeus,
    a tyrant like Pilate,
      an adultress in Samaria,
        a worshiper like Mary,
          a religious leader like Nicodemus,
            a fisherman like Peter,
              a turncoat like Judas,
                a Roman soldier, or even
                  a Jewish high priest.

He could listen to the charges of his worst enemies.

He could even accept the accusations of his dearest friends.

When Mary and Martha blamed him for their brother's death, he responded without a hint of defensiveness.

He could accept the rebuke of Peter without rejection.

He could receive the doubts of Thomas without feeling threatened.

He could mingle with all classes, all ages, and all races.

Jesus was totally comfortable with people.

Jesus was comfortable even with a hostile world.

He accepted those who rejected him.
He knew who was responsible for their hostility.
He knew the source of their unholy energies.
He knew why they hated him.
He met their accusations with silence.
He ignored their taunts.
He could rebuke Satan with authority.
He could cast out demons with power.
He could identify hypocrisy.
He could walk away from repeated threats on his life.
He could walk right into his most horrible hour

without hesitation. His confident stride carried
him toward, not away from, a cruel death.
He allowed men to flog him in silence.
He permitted them to beat him without response.
He let them place him on a cross.
He willingly permitted them to kill him.
He even allowed them to lay the "Light of the
World" in the total darkness of the tomb—and
through it all he asked but one thing—that they
be forgiven.
Jesus accepted even those who hated him.
Jesus was comfortable with a hostile world.

Jesus displayed acceptance and enjoyed acceptance.
He was totally comfortable in what was potentially history's most uncomfortable position.

I have often looked at the life of my Lord with not
only spiritual, mental, and physical admiration, but with
psychological admiration as well.

His life of balanced relationships—
His characteristic transparency—
His genuineness—
His ease with people—
His peace with himself—
What a model to emulate.
What a life to copy.
What an example to cherish and seek after.
Could I ever experience that sort of freedom?
Could I ever display that degree of acceptance?
Could I ever be that spiritually beautiful?

"I wanted to be so
genuine that I could
feel absolute and
total comfort with
myself, with God,
and with others.
I wanted to be REAL."

Chapter Five

"I Want to Be REAL"

I first started taking a long, hard look at myself when I was stuck in a deep, black hole of depression. From that position everything about myself was obscured, blurred, or completely invisible. Nothing looked good. Nothing looked real.

All of my neurotic little notions were magnified. They all appeared so big, so overpowering, that I was finding life with this ugly self becoming intolerable. I liked nothing about me and of course felt that everyone else shared the same opinion.

At about this time, a new message began coming from pulpits across the land. It was foreign; it was also suspect. The message was telling me to love myself.

At first it sounded good—especially to a person so engulfed by self-hate as i was. Yet I remember filtering that little four-letter word, self, through my mental concordance every time I had the opportunity. I had often taught that the flesh was nothing more than self spelled backwards with an added letter for emphasis, and that flesh, when used of man in his non-spiritual state, was an ugly word.

I began reading all I could find on the subject of self: Huxley, Niebuhr, Oppenheimer, John Dewey, Skinner, Maslow, Jourard, Jung, and of course Carl Rogers.

The whole theory of Carl Rogers is based on the need for self-acceptance. Rogers teaches that man's basic challenge is to understand himself and to accept himself. He states emphatically that no one can understand and accept himself until another has first understood him and accepted him as he is. Once we are understood and accepted by another, Rogers states, most of the neurotic little notions that bind us can be discarded and we can be comfortable with ourselves.

I became intrigued with all the ego defense mechanisms employed to protect myself from the frightening monsters of anxiety and guilt and inferiority. It seemed that Carl Rogers was talking about me.

As I read Rogers I agreed with him. I did not trust or accept myself to even be myself—that it was impossible for me to be what he calls "real" because I refused to allow myself the privilege of even owning my own feelings.

I was especially impressed with his many statements that suggest that no one can grow until he first accepts himself as he is.

Abraham Maslow states similarly that a lack of self-acceptance hinders growth, blocks knowledge, and stifles maturity.

It began to make sense to me that my obsession with self was a self-limiting problem. I spent so much time concentrating on thoughts of self that growth was impossible.

But "self-love" continued to bother me. Paul's letter to Timothy[1] describes self-love as one of the negative characteristics of man in the last days.

How could self-love be a spiritual goal when at the same time it is described as such an evil characteristic?

As I continued to pursue my own problem, the church's bookshelves began to fill up with books on self-image—self-esteem—self-acceptance—and even self-love. It soon became listed as humanity's number one need.

Dr. Nathaniel Branden, in his book, *The Psychology of Self-Esteem,* underscores its significance by stating that the desire for self-esteem is an urgent imperative. He insists that it is the single most significant key to a person's behavior.[2]

Dr. Robert Schuller, senior pastor of Garden Grove Community Church in Southern California, proposed the idea that the desire to achieve self-esteem is man's "ultimate will" and that what we want more than anything else in all the world is the awareness that we are worthy persons. He says, "Man is a primate driven by a hunger for self-esteem." He argues that "God made the human being to be great, glorious and proud."[3]

But did he? I wanted to understand myself, know myself, and ultimately be comfortable with myself, but the project still seemed to either be blown out of proportion or misdirected. And wasn't there more? Is it only self that needs acceptance? I seemed to be rejecting others nearly as much as myself. Where did they enter this complex picture?

It was during one of these bewildering times that Martha gave me a little book entitled, *The Velveteen Rabbit.*[4] Many have read this intriguing children's story—a fairy tale with all sorts of adult implications. I hadn't—I had not even heard of this delightful little book.

I looked for a long time at the illustrated cover—a cover that displayed the picture of a rabbit—a stuffed rabbit that was tattered and frayed—worn and torn from what appeared to be years of playful loving from an adoring child.

I opened the book with interest. Fairy tales were really not my style, and yet each word seemed to jump from the page with increasing fascination. I realized that somehow a stranger by the name of Margery Williams seemed to be writing a story about me.

The Rabbit with its velveteen covering had been a

Christmas gift to a boy who had long since stopped playing with it. It was shy, inferior, and neglected in favor of
the more superior and expensive toys that belonged to its
owner. It could not claim any uniqueness and felt itself
quite out-of-date. It was constantly plagued with feelings
of insignificance and loneliness. Its only friend was Skin
Horse, grown old and bald from years of constant attention. Skin Horse was considered wisest of all the toys in
the nursery.

One day as the Velevteen Rabbit was examining its
skin of cloth and insides of sawdust and feeling very sorry
for itself, it found itself lying near enough to Skin Horse
to ask a question. "What is REAL? Does it mean having
things that buzz inside you and a stick-out handle?"

I was stunned as I read that paragraph. From within
the covers of a little child's fairy tale, a sawdust-stuffed
rabbit had asked a question that to me was *the* question.
The question whose time had come. The question that
seemed to sum up all of the baffling and bewildering
struggles that I had been internalizing for so long. When
that make-believe rabbit in that children's fairy tale
asked, "What is REAL?" this grown man suddenly felt
large, moist tears coursing their way down his cheeks and
spattering those clean white pages.

Skin Horse responded that REAL isn't how you are
made—it's something that happens to you. It's something that happens when someone loves you for a long,
long time—really loves you. It's something that happens
slowly and sometimes painfully. It's something that seldom happens to fragile, insensitive people—it's something one becomes, but not before many years of constant
use have taken place. Usually REAL doesn't happen until
most of your hair has been loved off and your eyes have
dropped out. By then, however, it really doesn't matter
how you look—for when you are REAL you can't be ugly,
except to people who don't understand.

Skin Horse proceeded to tell Velveteen Rabbit how
years of loving had made him REAL and concluded by

saying "Once you're REAL you can't become unreal again. It lasts for always."

I read on, my attention riveted to the words before me, stopping only to wipe away the tears that would repeatedly blur the words.

Finally the day came, years later, when Velveteen Rabbit heard his owner say those truly magic words. It came after many long nights of sleeping on Boy's arm. Nights when Boy would snuggle close and talk to him through the long moonlight hours. It came long after his fur had become shabby and his tail unsewn and after all the pink had rubbed off his nose. It came after long days in the garden and rides in the wheelbarrow and picnics on the grass. It came at a most unexpected moment when Nana reached down into the bed one night to grab away the little rabbit, wet and dirty from the long day outside.

Boy resisted and Nana, after wiping the Rabbit off with a corner of her apron said, "Fancy all that fuss for a toy!" Boy sat up and reached for Velveteen Rabbit and said, "Give me my bunny! You mustn't say that. He isn't a toy. He's REAL."

That was all I could take. I stopped reading, closed the book, and began to sob. I felt foolish. Imagine a grown man crying over a child's fairy tale—and yet it was, at that moment, far more than a fairy tale. It was a statement—profound, clear, and powerful. A statement that I had been trying for years to make. A statement that I couldn't even wrap the right words around. It was saying what I wanted to be—what I wanted to feel. I wanted to be REAL. Real without fear of disclosure. I wanted to be so genuine that I could feel absolute and total comfort with myself, with God, and with others. I wanted to be REAL.

I sobbed through the night. Who could have known —who would have guessed that a little child's book, given by my wife, might be used to point straight to the heart of my problem. That little book put into clear, discernable language what it was that I was truly longing to experience. I just wanted to be REAL. That was all.

As I continued to look at the cover of that little children's book, question after question began to pour out of my perplexed soul.

> Does being REAL have anything to do with feeling accepted?
>
> Is genuineness a part of feeling totally comfortable with myself, God, and others?
>
> How does it happen?
>
> How long does it take?
>
> Is it really as painful as Skin Horse says?
>
> Is love really the all-important key that unlocks the door to my ugly brown prison house?
>
> Is it love that frees me of my cocoon?
>
> If so, whose love? What kind of love?
>
> Where is a love to be found that could ever be that freeing?

Chapter 5, Notes

1. 2 Timothy 3:2.
2. Nathaniel Branden, *The Psychology of Self-Esteem* (New York: Bantam Books, 1971), p. 110.
3. Robert H. Schuller, "The Theology of Self-Esteem," *The Saturday Evening Post*, May-June 1980, p. 44.
4. Margery Williams, *The Velveteen Rabbit, or How Toys Become Real* (New York: Doubleday, n.d.).

"It seems that the whole world is sharing my cocoon with me—that we're all feeling the same way about ourselves."

Chapter Six

"Why Do I Feel Inferior?"

How does one really get to know and understand and accept himself? How does one move from his threatening world of "phony" to the wonderful world of "real"?

Is self-acceptance as important as Carl Jung suggests when he says,

> Accepting of oneself is the essence of the moral problem and the acid test of one's whole outlook on life. That I feed the beggar, that I forgive an insult, that I love my enemy in the name of Christ—all of these are undoubtedly great virtues . . . but what if I should discover that the least among them all, the poorest of all the beggars, the most impudent of all the offenders, yes, the very fiend, himself—that these are in me, and I myself stand in need of the alms of my own kindness, that I, myself, am the enemy who must be loved—what then?[1]

As I continued to read, most psychologists were telling me that man is an enigma to himself—that he lacks the means of comparison for self-knowledge. He can distinguish himself from other animals but is completely lacking in criteria for self-judgment.

Most were saying that if I really wanted to understand myself, I must find someone who will listen to me, not judge me, but love me in spite of what I tell him. I must verbalize my thoughts, my feelings, my fears, and anxieties to someone I can completely trust.

Dr. Paul Tournier, Swiss psychiatrist and author, says,

> How beautiful, how grand and liberating the experience is when people learn to help each other. It is impossible to overemphasize the need humans have to be really listened to, to be taken seriously, to be understood. . . . No one can develop freely in this world and find a full life without feeling understood by at least one person. . . . He who would see himself clearly must open up to a confidant freely chosen and worthy of such trust.[2]

Rogers and Jourard were telling me the same thing —find a friend whom you can really trust and tell him everything.

I did.

It happened during the time of my deep depression. Dr. Emery Nester, psychologist and long-time friend, offered to listen, and I was finally willing to talk.

Self-disclosure came terribly hard at first. I had suppressed feelings, thoughts, and ideas for so long that to dredge them up and force them to the surface was not only difficult but downright painful.

I called these long hours "my trip to the womb." The process was more one of self-disclosure than psychoanalysis. Emery was very careful, in true Rogerian style, to make no value judgments, draw no conclusions, and offer no criticism. He just listened. Occasionally he would probe with an appropriate question or he would offer a brief but relevant comment, but mostly he just listened.

For the first time in my life, I was hearing myself as I

wrapped intelligible words around unintelligible thoughts and feelings.

I talked about my feelings of anxiety. I learned to describe just how they felt, when they were strongest, how they affected me. We then explored possible reasons for their existence.

An overwhelming sense of inadequacy consumed much of our conversation time together. It was a mystery to both of us how one who had experienced such success in life could continue to feel so inadequate.

We explored feelings of guilt. We found that while there was just cause for some, most of those feelings came from an inability to fully accept forgiveness.

Hostility was a big subject. How can one who professes love feel so hostile? We explored the frustrations and bitternesses that had accumulated through the years into such a large pile of unacceptable disappointments that they finally overpowered my feelings of love with outbursts of unrestrained anger.

I was anxious to know why the cocoon? Why was I so obsessed with the need for a covering to completely hide me from what I felt were the prying eyes of humanity?

Why did I feel so inferior? Was it inherent or acquired? Was it real or imagined? How did it display itself? When was it most evident? When was it least evident? When was it no problem at all?

What was the cause for such low feelings of self-worth? Who had told me directly or implied that I was of such little value? Martha had never implied this. My parents had never suggested it. No one in all my recollections had seriously promoted the idea. Where had such a notion originated?

"Decision-making comes so hard for me," I told Emery. I described how I would vacillate from one position to another, jump from one conclusion to another. I seemed to change my mind too often and for no apparent reason.

Where do the feelings of insecurity come from? I am loved, and yet feel that I could lose that love at any moment. I am respected, but feel that it's only temporary. I am trusted, but fear exposure. Why do I feel that my world is so tentative and my relationships so fragile? Why do I feel that life is one frightful balancing act on a tightrope with the constant, nagging fear of falling always haunting me?

Why do I feel so unloved? I don't know anyone who is more loved than I, and yet it's so difficult for me to feel loved—to enjoy love—to relax in the presence of love.

We explored these questions and more—in depth and in complete confidence—for more than a hundred hours. I talked and Emery listened, usually for no longer than an hour or two at a time. As I reached further and further back in time and deeper and deeper into that deep pile of suppressed feelings, some remarkable things happened.

I learned first of all that many of my feelings and thoughts and fears were quite common to all. I was not the only person confined to a cocoon. Many people spin webs. As a matter of fact, most of us hide in the very same cocoon, so absorbed with ourselves that we don't even notice each other.

I remember being deeply impressed with a fellow-member of a group therapy session during my stay in the Veterans Hospital. Bob was one of the most "all-together" people I had ever met. He was always impeccably dressed, poised, and confident. His deep, resonant voice sounded so magnificent—especially compared with what I felt was my own squeaky, high pitched vocal quality. He was successful in business, liked by others. When he spoke, everyone listened. When I spoke, it seemed that suddenly the whole world lost interest. He was tall and handsome. Alongside him I felt squat and ugly. I *felt* genuinely and totally inferior to him.

Following an extensive group therapy session one day, I finally summoned up all the courage I could muster, turned to Bob, and said, "Bob, how do I come through to you?" He looked down at me and asked in his authoritative and resonant voice, "What do you mean, how do you come through to me?" I stammered for a moment, rephrased my question and asked again, "Bob, what do you think of me? How do I appear to you? What kind of person do you think I am?"

Bob stopped, looking intently at me for a long time before answering. As he was framing just the right words, I noticed his eyes becoming moist, and finally, in a halting and hesitant manner, he said, "Don, I would give anything to be like you. I don't think I have ever met a man who has got it all together more than you. If ever I would pick a model after whom to pattern my life, you'd be the man."

I was stunned—speechless—bewildered. I suddenly saw beyond myself just long enough to realize that I was not all alone in my cocoon after all. I had company. There was one other person in this world who was struggling with the same feelings of inferiority as I—and he had been willing to admit it!

That one experience of awareness was freeing to me, and as I have opened my eyes even wider in the darkness of my little hiding place, I have become aware of other forms and figures crouched in their little corners, fearful of discovery. In fact, now it seems that the whole world is sharing my cocoon with me—that we're all feeling the same way about ourselves.

I learned something else. I learned that many of my fears were imagined. I have a vivid imagination and an alarming tendency to play mind reader. Often when I'm trying to determine what another person is thinking, I drift about as far away from reality as possible. I ascribe thoughts and motives to others that have no basis in fact whatever.

I am also sensitive. Sensitivity is one of the most important tools in my trade. I use it constantly. I am always looking for hidden signs of pain—seeking for subtle indications of hurts. I listen intently for words or innuendos that will unexpectedly expose another's hidden wounds so that I can move in close to become the healer.

All too often, however, this sensitivity backfires on

me, and *I* become the wounded. Grasping a misspoken word or a subtle look, I interpret it as a clever little dart thrown in my direction and designed to inflict pain on me, when that was not intended at all.

Even after all the helpful counseling sessions, though, I was finally forced to admit that this still wasn't enough.

The project had just begun.

I had learned that most of my prison was of my own making. Some of it was even an illusion.

I had learned that I was not the only prisoner. That was comforting, but didn't really set me free.

I had begun to spot some of the webs that bound me and found that some could even be loosened. Still others, however, held me tight.

I needed more than someone to listen to me.

I needed an authoritative, totally trustworthy voice to tell me what was really true about myself—a voice that was clear, concise, honest, and directive.

> If reality is so important—
> If genuineness is so vital—
> If acceptance is so necessary in order to experience a feeling of total comfort with myself, my God, my friends, and even my enemies—
> If this experience is as critical as everyone suggests—

then it *has* to be important to God. And if it's important to God, it must be discussed concisely somewhere in the great depository of Truth—the Scriptures.

Chapter 6, Notes

1. Carl Jung, quoted in Cecil Osborne, *The Art of Understanding Yourself* (Grand Rapids: Zondervan Books, 1967), p. 28.
2. Paul Tournier, quoted in John Powell, *why am i afraid to tell you who i am?* (Allen, Tex.: Argus Communications, 1969), p. 5.

———————

"I was amazed when I first realized just how psychologically precise the Bible really is."

———————

Chapter Seven

The Way Out

I came upon the solution quite by accident. I was doing an extensive study on the subject of church growth in Ephesians, when I became intrigued with one paragraph—three verses that for some strange reason I had failed to fully comprehend.

I was surprised to find four words, long overlooked, that when fully understood became the answer to my life's most baffling questions: How can I experience acceptance? How can I feel accepted? How can I be comfortable with myself, God, and others?

Four words provided me with the secret to right relationships—the means by which I could experience total comfort with others—the key to acceptance. Four simple but strategic words, tucked away in one of the Bible's most important chapters, actually described the way out of my cocoon. Those four words pointed me to the single, almost invisible thread that began the long, slow, unraveling process ultimately designed to free me.

The four words provide the explanation for Jesus' totally integrated personality. They are relational terms,

51

spiritual words, and psychological expressions. To the degree that I understand and employ these important concepts, I am able to enjoy the same delightful balance experienced by my Lord.

The problem with these words is that they are what I call "ho-hum" terms: words that are used so often, practiced so seldom, and defined with such vagueness that we're tired of trying to merely understand them—let alone practice them.

Each word, in itself, provides a gold mine of psychological and spiritual insight. Each word is loaded with the sort of verbal dynamic needed to release me from my bondage. Each word relates to the subject of acceptance. When understood and practiced, these words allow for the elusive privilege of being totally comfortable with myself and with others.

These words speak to the disabling problems of low self-esteem, hostility, fear, and rejection—those numbing warps in my personality that make comfortable relationships so difficult.

I was amazed when I first realized just how psychologically precise the Bible really is. The Bible not only describes and defines all those neurotic little notions I spoke of earlier, it also tells where they come from, how they are cultivated, why they continue to exist, and what is required to be relieved of them.

The four words are found in the Book of Ephesians, chapter 4, verse 2. They are a vital part of one of the most important passages on human relationship in Scripture. They describe the relational attitudes that were charateristic of Jesus Christ and are then expressed as the relational attitudes to be displayed by each believer. They are basic to spiritual unity and necessary to make any company of believers irresistibly attractive to the world.

The four life-changing words are—believe it or not—

Humility
Gentleness
Longsuffering
Forbearance

The entire passage reads:

> I, therefore, the prisoner of the Lord, entreat you
> to walk [or live] in a manner worthy of the calling
> with which you have been called [or worthy of the
> name Christian],
>
> with all *humility* and *gentleness*, with *patience*, showing
> *forbearance* to one another in love,
>
> being diligent to preserve the unity of the Spirit in
> the bond of peace.   Ephesians 4:1-3

Verse 1 states that these four terms characterized the
life of Christ.

Verse 2 exhorts us to employ them in our own lives.

Verse 3 makes them indispensable to the experience
of spiritual unity or oneness—the experience of feeling totally and wonderfully comfortable with ourselves and
others.

These four crucial words, located at the fountainhead
of Scripture's most illuminating passage on church growth,
describe four relational foundation stones. They are essen-
tial to the construction of a company of believers who are
comfortable with each other and profoundly attractive to a
lonely, withdrawn, isolated, imprisoned population—a
population that craves the companionship available in the
Christian community.

Do you realize that a company of believers potentially provides the only place on earth where a man can
be truly at peace with himself and with others? When this
peace is being experienced, it makes the church an ir-
resistible attraction to the outside world.

This peace, this oneness, is dependent upon a full
and complete understanding and application of the
meaning of only four words. Words that tell us how to be
totally comfortable with God, totally comfortable with a
hostile world, and totally comfortable with ourselves.
Fully accepted and fully acceptable.

The word *humility* or lowliness of mind *addresses the
problem of low self-esteem* and enables me to know myself
and accept myself as I really am.

The word *gentleness* or meekness *addresses the problem of hostility, inner rage, floating anger*—those bewildering, negative feelings that lash out at others, oftentimes for no apparent reason.

The word *long-suffering speaks to the fears* that come from living in the midst of a hostile world—a world that is committed to the elimination of the church.

The word *forbearance speaks to the problems of factions, of bigotry and bias, intolerance, impatience, and discrimination.*

In other words, these four life-changing words are basic to our understanding of how to get along with people!

Christianity, remember, is an experience of right relationships. Self-acceptance, self-esteem, is not my only problem. I must learn how to relate not only to myself, but also to God, to others, and to the world about me. These words tell me just how that's done, and they tell it in that order.

Whenever we begin talking about relationships, the strategy of Satan and the strategy of God are immediately brought into sharp focus.

Satan's strategy has always been to divide—to separate—to alienate. Satan is the author of loneliness since his plan has always been a plan of estrangement. He's the one, I'm sure, who coined the phrase, "irreconcilable differences." He invented the word "incompatible." His goal has always been that of division.

> He separated himself from God.
> He separated the angels from God.
> He separated man from God.
> He separated man from woman.
> He separated nation from nation.
> He separated earth from heaven.

He knows how to drive sharp and penetrating wedges between people. That's his program, and he's been uniquely successful.

I sat in the living room of a couple married nearly thirty years and watched and listened as they spat their venom at each other. Their young teenage son sat, white and silent, in a distant corner. Finally in exasperation, the wife said to her husband, "Do you know, John, what I wish you'd do? I wish you'd take your gun, put it to your head, pull the trigger, and kill yourself—only please do it in the garage, so I don't have to clean up the mess."

I've been a member in a local church meeting where a state police officer was called to keep the peace.

The story is told of a small church that wanted to buy an organ. The only problem was that there were those who wanted it and those who didn't. They argued long and bitterly over the purchase. Finally it was bought. They then argued over where to put it. Each week it was moved from one side of the little auditorium to the other. One Sunday, the congregation arrived to find their new organ missing. They searched the building to no avail. They hurled accusations back and forth but still were unable to locate the missing instrument.

Years later and quite by accident it was found—right where it had been all the time—in the church baptistry.

Satan's strategy is to separate, to alienate, and in so doing to totally frustrate the work of Christ in believers' lives.

I'm a peacemaker at heart, and I'm called to sit or stand often between two lonely, frightened people whose world has stopped turning because of their inability to relate properly to each other.

I have felt that same loneliness myself. I have experienced it with my wife, my children, my friends, and my church family. Satan swings his sledgehammer of hate and drives that wedge deep into the heart of a beautiful relationship.

I've often wished I could forget the times that I have spoken ill-timed, ill-advised, cruel, and cutting words to those I love the most. Words that can never be recalled and that can seldom be forgotten.

Satan's world is a powerful world—but a lonely one. The world is frantically searching for a place where it can be at peace with itself and comfortable with others—a place where it can experience true acceptance.

God's strategy is just the opposite of Satan's. His is a strategy of reconciliation—of unity and peace and oneness. Since sin began, God has been taking broken relationships and putting them back together again. God's program is to

> reconcile man to God,
> man to himself,
> man to woman,
> man to man,
> nation to nation, and
> earth to heaven.

God knows how to blunt Satan's wedges and ultimately force them out of a relationship, restoring the oneness. God is in the business of dispelling loneliness and creating a body of people who are at peace with themselves and with each other.

Four simple words can frustrate the strategy of Satan. Four words can dress believers in a garment so attractive and compelling the world is forced to stop and stare. Four words that can free us from the need and desire to spin any more webs or hide in our sheltering cocoon. The first word, *humility* or *lowliness of mind*, is designed to deal with the perplexing problem of self-acceptance.

"There is Someone who knows me—the Real me—the complex me—past, present, and future. He's already done a complete character profile on me in the Scriptures."

Chapter Eight

Someone Who Knows Me

Self-acceptance simply means to accept what is totally and actually true about myself.

There are varying opinions as to how the truth about self is finally learned.

It is true that man is an enigma to himself; man cannot fully comprehend himself.

I do not know the REAL me.

I, along with the rest of the world's confused, have spent my whole life in front of distorted mirrors as a part of a life-long comedy routine, trying to look either horribly ugly or wonderfully beautiful.

I am told that to fully understand myself I must find someone I trust and verbalize my feelings to that person.

I did that, and was relieved to find some significant relaxation from many of my internal pressures—but not all of them.

We are told to study our past, listen to our friends, seek competent counsel, or check with our family. I also found a great deal of help in reading books related to the subject.

But every human source of understanding was limited.

No one possessed the type of X-ray vision needed to read my mind.

No one was capable of feeling the true psychological pulse of my heart.

No one fully knew my past.

No one understood my present.

No one even pretended to comprehend my future.

Self-acceptance can never be achieved while drifting through the foggy, imprecise notions of a baffling secular humanism—a baseless philosophy of life that denies the fact of God, the reality of eternity, the existence of authority, the purpose for being, and the sanctity or indestructibility of human life.

There is only One Source of undistorted, undisputed truth.

There is only One who knows the total truth about me.

There is only One who loves me enough to reveal that truth to me.

The truth, the whole truth, and nothing but the truth can come from God and God alone. As the Hebrew poet asserted in Psalm 139:

> It is God who has searched me.
> It is God who has known me.
> It is God who knows when I sit down.
> It is God who knows when I rise up.
> It is God who understands my thoughts before I even think them.
> It is God who knows my directions before I even walk in them.
> It is God who is intimately acquainted with all my ways.
> It is God who knows it all.
> It is God from whom I cannot hide.
> It is God who formed me.
> It is God who made me.

It is God who plotted my whole existence before I was even born.

Those twelve statements qualify God to tell me who and what I am.

Just in case more evidence might be required to convince us of God's limitless credentials, the book of Job, chapters 38-41, reveals the infinite distance between man's understanding and God's.

God asks Job seventy questions, none of which Job can answer—all of which are basic knowledge to God.

The God-Man, Jesus, on numerous occasions displayed his ability to tell me the truth about myself.

It is said of Jesus in John 2:25:

"He did not need anyone to bear witness concerning man for He Himself knew what was in man."

No one needed to inform Jesus who would betray him—

"For Jesus knew from the beginning who they were who did not believe, and who it was that would betray Him" (John 6:64).

Do you remember the first time Jesus saw Nathaniel? They had never met. As Nathaniel approached, Jesus did a complete character profile on this total stranger by commenting, "Behold, an Israelite indeed, in whom there is no guile!"

When Jesus spoke to his critics in John 5:42, he spoke to all of humanity. He stated simply, "I know you."

There is Somebody who knows me—the real me—the complex me—past, present, and future. He has already done a complete character profile on me in the Scriptures.

He has painted a multi-dimensional portrait of me—one that displays me as I truly and really am.

And then he flashed a statement for all to see that provides the key to my prison door. He said,

"And you shall know the truth, and the truth shall make you free" (John 8:32).

If I want to know all about me, it's already written, word for word, in the Scriptures.

But if I want to become comfortable with myself, accept myself, learn to live with myself, get acquainted with the REAL ME, something more is required—and that something more is HUMILITY—genuine humility or "lowliness of mind" as some versions read.

Humility is the act of the will that takes truth, drives it down from the head to the heart, and translates it into experience. It's the means by which I not only get acquainted with the REAL ME, but it's the means by which I even become comfortable with the REAL ME. Humility is the divine path to self-acceptance.

"We cannot change,
we cannot move away
from what we are,
until we thoroughly
accept what we are."

Carl Rogers

Accepting . . . What God Says about Me

"I'll never be remembered for my humility," is a remark I often heard my father-in-law laughingly make in reference to himself. Yet, that's exactly the most outstanding memory I have of this man of God.

Humility is one of those abused little words that carries a different meaning to almost everyone who hears it spoken.

In pagan Greek it suggested someone who was small, slavish, silent, and grovelling.

The phrase "lowliness of mind," which I prefer to *humility,* to some suggests someone who walks around with a bowed head, downcast eyes, and folded hands. I think this is what Dad had in mind when he used the word, and he was right, for this austere, dignified, southern gentleman who preached with the power of an apostle Paul never displayed that sort of demeanor.

Humility is hard to define.

"Lowliness of mind" is far more graphic, and since it is used repeatedly in Scripture to describe such persons as Jesus in Matthew 11:29, the apostle Paul in Acts 20:19, and since it is required of all believers in Ephesians 4:2, it can't be all bad.

The word does not suggest that I make myself small —a suggestion often found in the word humility. It's a word, rather, that teaches me—

> Not to bow my head,
> but to bow my mind.

It means that I lower my mind and cause it to bow in full reverence and respect for divine truth.

Lowliness of mind, the first step toward freedom, the first door to self-acceptance, the first move in the direction of total comfort with myself, God, and others, says:

I ACCEPT ALL THAT GOD SAYS ABOUT ME
WITHOUT ARGUMENT.

This was the chief characteristic of Dad's life and ministry.

I counsel a lot. I'm amazed at the number of people who move from pastor to pastor, much like some do with medical doctors. They're seeking a second opinion—a third opinion—or ultimately that one professional opinion that agrees with their own.

Humility or lowliness of mind acknowledges but one opinion, and that's God's. His opinion is first, last, and final. His opinion is right, and humility not only acknowledges the fact, but acts in accordance with that truth.

All of the truth about me is found in Scripture, and humility agrees with all that the Scripture says about me. Humility, then, becomes the biblical imperative that addresses the problem of self-esteem, self-image, self-concept, and self-acceptance.

It's the word that, when understood, tells me how to find the REAL ME.

It's the word that paves the way to ultimately becoming comfortable with myself.

The REAL ME is found in the Scriptures. It's in the Bible that I am fully and correctly described.

God's word addresses the disabling problem of low self-esteem.

David Seamands described low self-esteem as Satan's deadliest weapon—a weapon of the enemy that

> paralyzes my potential,
> destroys my dreams,
> ruins my relationships, and
> sabotages my Christian service.[1]

Dr. James Dobson listed ten sources of depression in marriage. Among these ten was low self-esteem. Fifty percent of the respondents rated it as problem number one. Eighty percent of the respondents listed it among the top three on their lists.

Humility speaks to this need. It tells me that if I want an objective, honest answer to who and what I am and why, then I must ACCEPT ALL THAT GOD SAYS ABOUT ME WITHOUT ARGUMENT.

A classic example of humanity's profile is found in the Book of Ephesians, chapter 2, verses 1-7. It explicitly tells the awful and wonderful truth about me, past, present, and future.

It not only tells the truth about me, but also the truth about you. In fact, we're allowed in this passage to look over the shoulder of God into the heart of all humanity—and surprise! We all look alike.

This passage is humanity's great equalizer. It eliminates words like *spiritual advantages* and *spiritual disadvantages*.

It erases words like *inferiority* and *superiority* in the spiritual realm.

It places us all under one great umbrella of Truth as look-alikes, act-alikes, and be-alikes.

These verses tell us that:

WE ALL HAD THE SAME PROBLEM (v. 1)

"And you were dead in your trespasses and sins."

We were *all* "dead in trespasses and sins." The word *dead* means more than just the absence of life; it means more than to be unresponsive and insensitive; it means to be actually and totally separated from the source of all life, which is God himself.

It means not only physical death or even emotional death, but spiritual death.

Humanity's obituary notice is carried in Genesis, chapter 3, and is explained in the Book of Romans:

> Therefore, just as through one man sin entered into the world, and death through sin, and so death spread to all men, because all sinned (5:12).

The infectious disease of death has spread through the entire human race.

This death or separation from God was caused by trespassing or crossing over the boundaries of God's law and by sin, or failing to live up to God's standard.

Since there are no degrees of death—nor degrees of life—one is either alive or dead. That means that no one has any advantage over me in this respect.

> I had no advantage over any other.
> I was dead.
> You were dead.
> Death is the great equalizer.
> We were all bound by the same limitation—
>   infected with the same hideous disease—
>   laid low by the same giant problem.
> We were all dead!

The chief characteristic of death is total helplessness. None of us could move ourselves in any direction, much less the direction of the Source of life.

Spiritual death ultimately invades every part of our being. It displays itself in varying states of emotional death: depression, restlessness, guilt, negativism, hopelessness, fear, and hate.

Just as a dead body has discernible characteristics so does a dead spirit.

Spiritual death is the sole cause of physical death, which is the universal consequence of sin. We were all dead and still are dead, as long as we remain separated from the life-source, which is God himself.

Have you ever noticed how lifelike a mortician can make a dead person appear? There is very little that's repulsive or ugly about a corpse at a funeral.

In our state of spiritual death we do the same.

We try desperately to appear lifelike and alive.

Cocoons are quite popular among the spiritually dead.

Nevertheless, God says that the REAL me—before Jesus Christ entered my life—was dead.

Self-acceptance acknowledges this truth as a fact of life.

Lowliness of mind states that I accept all that God says about me without argument—even if it appears untrue.

WE ALL HAD THE SAME LORD (v. 2)

> in which you formerly walked according to the course of this world, according to the prince of the power of the air, of the spirit that is now working in the sons of disobedience.

The second thing God says about me—THE REAL ME—past, is that I was completely under the control and influence of demonic energy.

I was a Satanist.

The energizing spirit that controlled my thoughts as well as my actions was the same energizing spirit that controls the entire world system—the prince who rules over earth—Satan, himself.

My first experience of exorcism was both awesome and frightening. After hours of spiritual struggle I finally witnessed the freeing of a twenty-seven year old man from the domination of Satan.

The long, hard battle wearied and wounded us both.

I was feeling quite proud of what I mistakenly thought was my accomplishment. I began telling the fascinating story in vivid detail every chance I got.

I took my new friend to Multnomah School of the Bible in Portland, Oregon. As we walked into Dr. John Mitchell's office, I said, with carnal pride, "Dr. Mitchell, I want you to meet my new friend and brother in Christ— he is a former Satanist."

Without a moment's hesitation, Dr. Mitchell

responded with, "Weren't we all?" He proceeded to talk to us without any further comment in regard to my friend's former life.

"Weren't we all!" Yes, we were—all of us—Satanists, completely under Satan's power and control.

I was a pawn of Satan, helpless to have any say whatever about how I would live.

Lowliness of mind says I believe all that God says about me without argument—even if it's very uncomplimentary.

WE ALL HAD THE SAME LIFE STYLE (v. 3)

> Among them we too all formerly lived in the lusts of our flesh, indulging the desires of the flesh and of the mind, and were by nature children of wrath, even as the rest.

The REAL ME, past, lived to satisfy only one person—me. I was indulgent and sensual—interested in making certain that I had anything and everything I wanted. Greed and selfishness motivated me completely. I had only my interests at heart.

My concern for others was displayed primarily as a means of getting something for myself.

The human tendency to spin webs around ugly reality is at its peak right here. All of us, before coming to Christ, did our best to hide the fact that we were totally selfish and self-centered.

Carl Jung has said that only when a person understands the duality of his nature—his capacity for evil as well as good—can he begin to understand and cope with those who threaten him.

Only when an individual discovers his true inner nature can he accept the gift of meaningful life from God.

Carl Rogers has said that only when a person accepts himself as he really is, does he have the capacity to change.

Verse 3 paints a very unflattering picture of the REAL ME, and I must confess that when I first began taking a long look in that undistorted mirror of self, I wasn't sure that I really wanted to know more.

Lowliness of mind means accepting all that God says about me without argument, even if it's bad.

WE ALL HAVE RECEIVED THE SAME LOVE (v. 4)

But God, being rich in mercy, because of His great love with which He loved us . . .

Of all the insights into self-acceptance, this one may be the most crucial.

Have you noticed how many times I have stated the same concept over and over again?

"No one can accept himself until he is first accepted by another."

I cannot love me unless you do.

The rejected are never able to experience total comfort with themselves or with others.

Do you remember Abraham Maslow's hierarchy of needs?

I was stunned when I first saw them years ago. There was the answer to my perpetual question: Why was professional growth—personal growth—so slow, so difficult?

Maslow states that:

Before there can be growth, there must be self-esteem.

Before there can be self-esteem, there must be love.

Before there can be love, there must be security.

Before there can be security, physical needs must be met.

He outlines them in this order:

Growth

Self-esteem

Love

Security

Physical Need

As long as I'm hungry—I'll never feel secure.

As long as I'm insecure—I'll never feel loved.

As long as I'm unloved—I'll never have self-esteem.

As long as I lack self-esteem—I'll never grow.

My problem focused immediately. My inability to accept love—to feel love—to experience and enjoy love—made it impossible to accept myself.

Notice the critical moment in Scripture where God injects the miracle potion—LOVE.

He has just described us as separated, Satanists, and sensual, and now he pauses to tell us that he loves us anyway.

He describes the heavenly rescue operation, prompted only by love, that was designed to

> bring us to life,
>> snatch us from the clutches of Satan, and
>>> preserve us from the weakness of self.

You'd better read that verse again.

> But God, being rich in mercy, because of His great love with which He loved us . . .

I get a catch in my throat every time I read this passage.

I get another catch in my throat every time I hear Bill Gaither's little chorus:

> I am loved. I am loved. I can risk loving you
> For the One who knows me best, loves me most.

All the nasty things God says about me in the first three verses of Ephesians, chapter 2, would tend to make me think that God could not love me—ever.

But he did, and he does.

Lowliness of mind states that I believe all that God says about me without argument—even if it's unbelievable.

Believe it—God loves me, anyway.

WE HAVE ALL RECEIVED THE SAME LIFE (v. 5)

> . . . even when we were dead in our transgressions, made us alive together with Christ (by grace you have been saved) . . .

The REAL ME has been revived, resuscitated, restored—brought back to life. God has devised his own method of cardio-pulmonary resuscitation that reaches beyond the organ of the heart to the human spirit.

The spirit of man that went limp when Adam sinned has been made alive. This aliveness, this new life, is the result of a fusion with the source of eternal life—Jesus Christ.

It's not accomplished by a wand or with a touch.

It's not like the resurrection of a Lazarus who was called out of death or a widow's son who was commanded to live or even a priest's daughter who was lifted out of death by the tender hand of Jesus.

This aliveness is not just a change of mind or a change of direction.

It's not a new-found allegiance or a redefined dedication.

It's the actual merging of two persons—one dead and one alive.

It's the result of the eternal, indestructible life of the ever-living, never-dying Christ, moving right into my being.

It's the result of my never-ending death being drawn right into his never-ending life and being eternally conquered.

My death is swallowed up by his life.

My death is exchanged for his life.

We two, Christ and I, become one.

Christ lives in me and I live in him.

We are so inseparable and so indistinguishable that when God the Father sees us, he sees us not as two but as one.

That's what is meant in verse five when it says, "made us alive together with Christ."

It's interesting to note right here that the same Satan who works overtime to convince spiritually dead people that they are alive also expends a similar amount of demonic energy to convince spiritually alive people that they are still dead.

At age nine it really wasn't difficult for me to accept the fact that I needed to accept Jesus.

What *was* difficult was to accept the fact that Jesus had accepted me.

I struggled with uncertainty for ten frightening years before I was able to believe that I had been brought back to life.

The unmistakable signs of spiritual life were everywhere. The most significant sign of life was my fear of spiritual death. Dead people have no awareness of their state whatsoever. Only the spiritually alive are capable of even expressing concern over their spiritual welfare.

I completely ignored this obvious sign of my aliveness.

The fact of life is just as real as the fact of death.

Since there are no degrees in death or in life, no one is more dead or more alive than anyone else.

Life, like death, is a great equalizer. The passage of time doesn't make me any more alive than I am at the moment of my spiritual birth.

Even the process of maturing contributes nothing to my aliveness.

Outside of Christ, I could not be any more dead than I was.

In Christ, I cannot be any more alive than I am.

The REAL ME is alive with the eternal, indestructible life of Christ—a life that can never again know the kind of death and separation it once knew.

Be sure you don't overlook the little word *grace* in that verse. That little word, big with meaning, makes it clear that the process of becoming alive is something accomplished by God alone—it's a free, totally undeserved gift given to anyone who is willing to accept the whole truth just as God states it.

Lowliness of mind states that I accept all that God says about me without argument, even if it's astonishingly wonderful.

WE HAVE ALL RECEIVED THE SAME STATUS (v. 6)

> . . . and raised us up with Him, and seated us with Him in the heavenly places, in Christ . . .

Since Jesus and I are inseparable and indistinguishable in our spiritual life, I am not only alive, I am already comfortably positioned with Christ in the very same place Jesus is located today. I am already located spiritually where someday I'll be located physically—in the very presence of God the Father. This is in a place beyond the reach of Satan, beyond the possibility of loneliness, and beyond the threat of weakness.

I am already positioned for perpetual peace and everlasting security.

I am located in a spot that is not tentative.

I am assured by a promise that is not ambivalent.

I am surrounded by forces that are indestructible.

I am as secure for all eternity as is Jesus,
    as close to God as is Jesus, and
        as acceptable to God as is Jesus.

Jesus is heaven's status symbol, and since you and I both are located in him and with him, there will never be any class distinction or segregation or discrimination. In Christ we are all on the top rung of the heavenly ladder, and from that perch we'll enjoy forever together.

Lowliness of mind states that I accept all that God says about me without argument, even if it's beyond comprehension.

WE WILL ALL SHARE THE SAME PURPOSE (v. 7)

> . . . in order that in the ages to come He might show the surpassing riches of his grace in kindness toward us in Christ Jesus . . .

The REAL ME is in store for something that's both special and spectacular. In the future—the eternal future—God is going to spend his time heaping blessing after blessing upon me and pause only occasionally to show me off to all his creation as a trophy of his mighty power and his wonderful grace.

Eternity will be like one long ticker-tape parade, where we will be the spectacle for all the angelic beings to behold.

We will be the freed hostages that will be displayed as

a lasting tribute to the strategy and wisdom of God.

We will be the marvel of the ages to come. Heaven's hottest commodity. God's greatest achievement. Time's most spectacular miracle.

The REAL ME is going to be SOMEBODY forever.

Lowliness of mind states that I accept all that God says about me without argument even if it, excuse the expression, boggles my mind.

The Word of God describes the REAL ME and the REAL YOU.

It gives us a realistic, objective, honest appraisal of ourselves.

It's discouraging at first, but it directs us to the means by which we can be changed.

It describes my wonderful status in Jesus Christ, and promises me that it's going to get even better.

It singles no one out as better or worse—it places us all under the same umbrella of divine truth and enables us to ultimately accept ourselves as we truly are.

If God can accept me—and he does—knowing what he knows, then I can accept me.

If God can love me—and he does—knowing what he knows, then I can love me.

If God esteems me as he esteems his son, Jesus, then I can give myself the esteem I truly deserve.

That esteem is not a haughty arrogance that presumes superiority—it is rather a grateful serenity that has finally found peace and comfort with itself.

The truth of God frees me! It eliminates the need for spinning webs of unreality. It allows me the privilege of breaking free of my cocoon and enables me to fly with ease and grace and magnificent beauty above and beyond all the restraints of an unbelieving heart.

Chapter 9, Notes

1. David A. Seamands, *Healing for Damaged Emotions* (Wheaton, Ill.: Victor Books, 1981), p. 50.

———————————

"In order to be
comfortable with God,
I must know my God
as he really is."

———————————

Chapter Ten

Accepting ... How God Deals with Me

I just took another look at my woolly friend. I study him often—in fact, I find myself getting a little anxious, wondering if that moth will ever break free.

From all appearances, nothing has changed. The cocoon shows no sign of life or struggle. There's no indication that soon something beautiful will emerge, no hint that something magnificent and alive will climb out of something that appears so ugly and lifeless.

It took a long time for that little larva to wrap itself so tightly and completely. It takes a long time to break free.

If you're getting discouraged with the bindings that have caused you to go into hiding—be patient. The process of gaining freedom may seem frightfully slow, but that freedom is certain once you've begun your struggle.

Believe me! I know.

Part of the process must include learning to feel comfortable, not only with myself, but also with God. Accepting God for who he is and feeling accepted by God are indispensable to the freedom we crave.

The second word in Ephesians 4:2 addresses this

worthy project. In your revised version it reads *gentleness*. In the King James the word is *meekness*. I prefer the word meekness even though it also has suffered some terrible abuse in translation.

I read a sign on a billboard the other day that said, "Meekness is weakness." Modern society views meekness as a lack of aggressiveness, or assertiveness, and rejects it with contempt.

True meekness, however, *is not weakness*. It is an inner strength that responds positively to all the happenings of life.

Meekness is a g. ace of soul that produces acceptable responses to even unacceptable circumstances.

Meekness is the spirit's positive response to negative experiences.

As lowliness bows its mind to the truth of God, meekness bows its will to the dealings of God.

It is the gentle, mild, undisputing, unabrasive response to whatever God allows to take place in my life.

Meekness says:

> I ACCEPT ALL OF GOD'S DEALINGS WITH ME WITHOUT RESISTANCE OR BITTER-NESS.

Jesus, in Matthew 11:29, described himself as meek (KJV).

Paul, in 1 Corinthians 4:21, says, "I came to you in meekness" (KJV).

Timothy, in 1 Timothy 6:11, is instructed to serve in meekness (KJV).

Wives in 1 Peter 3:4 are encouraged to display meekness.

Meekness in Galatians 5:23 is a fruit of the Spirit.

It's obvious from all the biblical emphasis on the word that meekness is a *positive* quality—not weakness, but strength.

One of the classic Old Testament illustrations of meekness is found in the life story of one of history's best-known sufferers, a man by the name of Job.

In one day Job lost everything he owned, 7000 sheep, 3000 camels, 500 yoke of oxen, and 500 female donkeys. In one day this rich man's world collapsed. He lost it all. In addition to his material loss, he was forced to take charge of the funeral arrangements and bury all ten of his children—all in one day (Job 1). All the heartbreaks of a lifetime were compressed into one twenty-four hour period, without even the privilege of time to heal the wounds.

How did he respond? Job 1:20-22 says,

> Then Job arose and tore his robe and shaved his head, and he fell to the ground and worshiped. And he said, "Naked came I from my mother's womb, and naked I shall return there. The Lord gave and the Lord has taken away. Blessed be the name of the Lord." Through all this Job did not sin nor did he blame God.

That's meekness. Job accepted all of God's dealings with him without resistance or bitterness—at first anyway.

As Job's story continues and as the pressures of pain and loss intensify, his display of meekness begins to waver.

Job complains,
     questions,
          criticizes,
               demands an explanation, and
                    pleads to die.

At the conclusion of his chronicle of suffering, Job confesses that his negative responses to negative experiences were the result of his limited knowledge of God.

Job, like most of us, knew God secondhand. His training had been thorough, his instruction had been complete, but his knowledge was academic.

An academic knowledge of God, one that's complete with all the right answers to all the right questions is fine for the classroom, but it will never suffice in life's living room.

In seminary I completed all of my biblical and systematic theology classes with superior grades, but I still didn't know God.

I knew about God—but I didn't know God.

Like Job, I had heard of him with the hearing of the ear—I had all the hearsay insights that I could handle.

I could define the terms, describe the relationships, and list the attributes. Like Job, however, my understanding of God was pitifully limited. I hadn't seen him with the seeing of my eyes.

Moses had the same problem. He had spent eighty years in a God-culture, knew his Jewish catechism, later even wrote his own Jewish history book, but when he stood beside that burning acacia bush at the base of Mt. Horeb, he suddenly realized that he hadn't even entered theological pre-school.

Moses did not know God.

Neither did Isaiah nor Ezekiel nor Daniel nor Jeremiah. Nor do we, until we encounter him personally in one of life's unexpected moments.

Knowledge of God is forged out of the furnace of life, formed on the anvil of experience, and oftentimes shaped with the hammer of pain.

My knowledge of God has only grown in proportion to my encounters with life—real life—hard life—cruel life—sometimes painful life. The most positive growing times have been amidst the most negative experiences.

As I am writing this, Martha and I are engulfed in another of life's baffling encounters, one that's downright painful.

After ten and a half happy years at Hinson Baptist Church in Portland, we're being asked to leave. Not by the church, but by God. We're being asked to leave our home, our children, our grandchildren, my eighty-six-year-old mother, my brothers and sister, all of our lifelong friends, our security, and this beautiful city, which we dearly love.

Not only that, we're being asked to go to a strange country, a different culture, an unknown people, and even a new denomination.

God is asking us, in these best years of our lives, years that are fast approaching retirement, to do something that feels strangely like starting all over again.

We feel a little like Abraham being asked to leave Ur of the Chaldees. The only difference being that Illinois—from my present vantage point—bears little resemblance to the Promised Land.

Our knowledge of God is being stretched again. We know enough about him to know when it is that he's speaking, and what it is that he is saying. We know enough about him to know our Sovereign God has a sovereign plan—one that we may or may not understand someday.

We know enough about him to realize the importance of obeying him. What we do not know is the exact, unique, wonderful, personalized, tailor-made reason for this bewildering request.

We're displaying meekness—oh, there's a little kicking and screaming going on—some tears and some apprehension—lots of questions—but we are meekly responding to the sovereign call of God.

You see, meekness says I accept all of God's dealings with me without resistance or bitterness.

As lowliness demands that I get to know the truth about myself, meekness requests that I get to know the truth about God.

Meekness sees God in every circumstance of life—not always causing it, but at least allowing it.

Meekness accepts the fact that God is sovereign, in control, and free to act in our behalf in any way he pleases.

Meekness truly believes that nothing can touch the child of God without first having gained the permission of our heavenly Father.

Meekness sees God actively involved in my polio.

Meekness sees God playing a major role in my four-year depression.

Meekness bows before a sovereign God in the death of our son.

Meekness views God as a part of every disappointment as well as appointment.

Meekness sees God in my failures as well as in my successes.

A seminary student stopped by the other day with twelve questions he wanted to ask. Paul had been a successful business man prior to his call to the ministry. He was well on the way to his first million and probably felt, like most of us, that his response to God's call would result in even greater prosperity. Instead, just the opposite had happened. And now he was almost penniless.

So he began asking me his questions:

1. Does following Jesus have to be so hard?
2. Why doesn't God answer prayer?
3. Why is seminary so hard?
4. Why do I have the impression that I'm just beating my head against a wall?
5. Why—

I stopped him right there. "No more questions," I said. "I'm not sure that I can answer even one that you've asked so far. I do know, Paul, that there are times when following Jesus seems awfully hard, and I, too, wonder why God is so slow to answer prayer. Seminary was hard for me, too, and at times I felt that my head was permanently damaged from the beatings it took."

As we talked, we both began to weep, for we were both feeling the struggles of an aggressive self-will against the contrary plans of a sovereign God.

"The problem can't be with God, Paul, it has to be with us. God's will is never hard except to an obstinate, rebellious spirit. When Jesus said, 'Take my yoke upon you and learn of me, for my yoke is easy and my burden is light,' he was telling us that serving him was never meant to be grievous and hard. Yokes are shaped to provide no discomfort whatever to the shoulders of the oxen. Yokes only hurt when the animal resists."

"That's the way it has always been in my life. The will of God is only unbearably painful when I resist it."

With those words, Paul buried his head in my shoulder and wept. He finally said, "Thanks, Pastor, for telling me like it really is. I think I can handle it now—no more questions."

Meekness says I accept all of God's dealings with me without resistance or bitterness.

Another beautiful display of meekness is found in Philippians, chapter 2. In the passage beginning with verse 5, we are told to:

> Have this attitude in yourselves which was also in Christ Jesus, who, although He existed in the form of God, did not regard equality with God a thing to be grasped, but emptied Himself, taking the form of a bond-servant, and being made in the likeness of men. And being found in appearance as a man, He humbled himself by becoming obedient to the point of death, even death on a cross.

This passage describes Jesus climbing down the ladder of self-interest—that's meekness on display as he volitionally displays commitment and compliance with the sovereign wisdom of his holy Father.

Meekness is heard in the form of singing as Paul and Silas accepted imprisonment in Philippi as a circumstance that is painful but providential.

Meekness is seen on a barren island as John the apostle bows to worship after his banishment to Patmos.

Meekness is the word that challenges the single person who wants to be married or the married person who wants to be single.

Meekness is the word that addresses the disappointment of a missionary who is denied a visa, a student who is declined admission, the businessman whose resumé is rejected, the parents who find themselves childless, the athlete who gets injured, the Christian whose business fails, the investor who loses his life savings. Meekness is being able to say, "Thank you, Father," when all that's been received has been a disappointment.

Negative responses to divinely permitted pressure

situations can be terribly destructive.

One Sunday evening I was called to sit between two members of my church as a peacemaker. I had been struggling with them for months, trying to find an acceptable solution to a very complex problem. I was tired, irritable, and genuinely displeased that this conference was tacked onto the end of a wearying day. I did not display my anger in their presence. I suppressed it—restrained it—sat on it—very successfully. It didn't show—but it was there.

As I was driving home, I passed Martha's Datsun sitting alongside the freeway, empty. I stopped, backed up, and found the doors locked and the parking lights dimmed from a near-dead battery.

I was angry because she had obviously run out of gas. I was doubly angry because the battery had run down. I was uncontrollably angry a few moments later when she drove up with a stranger and a can of gas. I was sure I was going to be "gouged" beyond my ability to pay. It turned out that it cost me nothing.

I poured the gas into the tank, vainly tried to start the engine, and finally decided to get behind her and push the car to a safer location. I explained what we were about to do, where we would turn, and when. I failed to explain that she needed to turn on the key in order to unlock the steering wheel. When I started pushing her, rather than steer toward the frontage road, she began heading for the middle of the freeway, with its concrete divider. We both stopped just in time.

I got out of my car, slammed the door, stormed up to her front window and began delivering a tirade. When I was finished, I asked her, "Why didn't you turn onto the frontage road?" She explained, "I'm sorry, I didn't know to turn on the ignition key. The steering wheel was still locked." Again I dumped my anger on her. After a few moments I saw a worried, embarrassed look in her eyes and heard words I'll never forget, "I'm your wife, remember?"

She forgave me—I've never really forgiven myself.

I've always felt that it was a classic example of misdirected anger. I wasn't really angry at Martha, I was angry at those two men who had consumed so much of my time and energy. But, no, not really. The truth is I was angry at God for allowing that long and tiring conference to take place.

Meekness sees God in every circumstance of life and meekness says I accept all of God's dealings with me without resistance or bitterness.

Had I responded to that pressure experience with meekness, I would have spared my wife from a painful wound and myself from a haunting memory.

One of my close friends has recently lost his wife, his health, his mobility, his physical independence, and his purpose for living. He is in a constant depression.

As I sat with him not long ago, he again expressed his disgust with the nursing home, the food, the staff, with himself, and with God for not answering his prayer to die.

"Are you angry with God?" I asked him.

He laughed with embarrassment. "Of course not," he said, "I would never get angry with God."

"Yes, you would," I replied, "and I think you are. Everything that's happened in your life this past year has been allowed by God and you don't like it. Isn't it possible that you are truly angry with God?"

Hebrews 12:15 warns us of the bitterness that spills over and infects many. I call it "floating anger." It's an anger that we're not even aware of, but every once in a while it erupts, usually inflicting wounds on unsuspecting and innocent victims and leaving piles of clutter and debris in the lives of many.

I can get rid of "floating anger" by acknowledging its presence and asking God's forgiveness for improperly responding to one of life's painful experiences. We really don't grow without pain, you know—in fact, pain is indispensable to growth. Pain, if it produces growth, is worthy of praise. Pain, like it or not, often becomes our best friend. God knows just how much pain we can stand and for how long and he knows just how to use it to cause a gentle spirit to emerge. God calls that gentle spirit meekness.

I was speaking in Denver during the time I was doing the word study in Ephesians, chapter 4. I worked late one night on the word meekness, finally defined it as you see it in this chapter, and then left it lying on the desk in my motel.

When I returned to my room the next day, I was just opening my door when a housekeeper came up from behind, asked me if I was Rev. Baker, and then threw her arms around me and began to cry.

I was stunned—I'd never seen the woman before in my life—until she began to explain.

"I'm married to a preacher," she said, "who has not been walking with God. In fact, he has made my life totally miserable. Last week I left him, and I determined I would never go back to him—until I read your definition for meekness. I knelt down beside your bed and asked God to forgive me for thinking I knew what was best for my life. I've already called my husband, and he's picking me up after work. We're going home."

Meekness seldom comes easily, for life is filled with disappointments. The only way that I have been able to experience any relief from the pain of denied self-interest is by getting better acquainted with God.

In order to be comfortable with God I must know my God—as he really is.

The information can't be secondhand, the evidence can't be hearsay. It must be gained from the depository of truth, the Scriptures, and applied in the crucible of life. To know God requires the marriage of truth to life's experiences.

It's such a freeing feeling to know that nothing can happen in my life without first having gained the permission of God.

A little blind girl was seated on her daddy's lap on the front porch when a long-time friend of the family quietly climbed the front steps, winked at his friend and then grabbed the blind daughter from her daddy's arms, ran down the steps and up the street.

He stopped abruptly, startled because the girl had made no effort to struggle or cry out. "Why aren't you frightened?" he asked. "You didn't know who had you in his arms." "I didn't have to know," she answered. "My daddy knew, and that was enough for me."

Meekness is the act of relaxing with any circumstance—knowing that our Father fully understands.

Meekness accepts all of God's dealings with me without resistance or bitterness and enables me to feel comfortable with God.

Meekness frees me from the cocoon of fear, the bondage of hostility, and the darkness of uncertainty. Meekness frees me to live in an expansive universe with the certainty that God is God of all and that every event of my life is under his sovereign control.

Meekness can be summed up in a single passage of Scripture—one that Martha and I have tried to live by all our lives.

> And we know that God causes all things to work together for good to those who love God, to those who are called according to His purpose (Romans 8:28).

"God's most powerful weapon on earth is a Christian who, when threatened or harmed, refuses to retaliate."

Chapter Eleven

Accepting . . . How Man Deals with Me

Lowliness of mind allows me to be comfortable with myself.

Meekness enables me to be comfortable with my God.

Longsuffering, the third of this little foursome of divine graces, permits me to find some semblance of serenity in a hostile world—a serenity that's uncharacteristic to us humans.

The world, especially when it's experiencing one of its periodic fits of anger, can be a very intimidating place to live.

For the world is a system that is

ruled by Satan,
    inhabited by demons,
        built on greed,
            fostered by hate, and
                bent on destruction.

It's a system whose total environment has been polluted by sin.

Its inhabitants resent the presence of Christians.

Its goal is to eliminate God and good, as it attempted to eliminate Christ.

The believer is an unwelcome resident. His very presence is a constant reminder of the vast moral difference between God and man. The resentment is greatest whenever he attempts to influence or even change his environment for Christ.

I collided head-on with the world system a few years ago when I led the evangelical community in an attempt to expose a gay activist takeover of Oregon politics in 1980.

Hinson Church is in the midst of a neighborhood strongly influenced by politics. Many of the residents are homosexuals and lesbians or are sympathetic to them. The homosexual community in Portland claims to be 100,000 strong and has threatened to take control of the city.

I must be careful here to explain that we have an active ministry to homosexuals and their families—and that we do not reject or oppose the individual homosexual. We are, however, opposed to the practice, especially when it attempts to dominate a community.

I authored a letter, signed by seven other influential church leaders, that listed all the local, state, and national candidates that were supported by the gay community. I stated the biblical position on homosexuality and encouraged the evangelical community to study the endorsements carefully before casting their votes.

The letter was distributed state-wide to more than 300,000 persons. The outcome of the election was heartening.

The response of the world-system was frightening.

I was maligned, abused, and threatened. Damage was done to the church buildings and its vehicles. Tires were slashed, graffiti began appearing on the walls. Foul-smelling chemicals were sprayed on the shrubs and sidewalks surrounding the church, permeating the entire building during the Sunday services.

I was intimidated and I withdrew.

The campaign was successful, but I hadn't expected the avalanche of hate that poured down upon me and my church family.

I wanted to turn in the direction of a full-scale retreat or gather my forces for all-out war.

My perplexity over what I had done was heightened as I watched the walls of hostility being erected between me and the very people that I wanted so desperately to help.

I began carefully studying the scriptural incidents that seemed to parallel mine:

> John the Baptist's public indictment of King Herod for his immorality;
>
> Jesus' rebuke of religious leaders for their hypocrisy;
>
> Stephen's address to traditional Judaism, shaming them for their lifelessness and unbelief;
>
> Peter's public accusation of a religious system that crucified Christ;
>
> Paul's constant warnings against false doctrine and impurity;
>
> John's scenario of the future that predicted the ultimate collapse of the total world system.

All of these men lived in a hostile world.

All of them addressed the evils of their present age.

All of them suffered persecution or death or both for their views.

None of them retaliated or sought revenge. All of them influenced their generation—and the generations to come—by their passive response to hostility.

I'm a war veteran. I'm not a pacifist, by nature or by doctrine. I'm a member of a generation that has grown up with a John Wayne mentality. I was taught to shoot by members of the National Riflemen's Association, and have studied ways to defend myself and the members of my family.

Friends and even members of my church have joined

survivalist organizations and stockpiled food, guns, and ammunition, in preparation for the coming world collapse. I have been urged by many to do the same.

I have strongly resisted and insistently refused, not because of my courage, but because of my convictions— convictions that are still in the formative stage, but growing. Convictions that state that:

> Hostility breeds hostility;
> the believer's true life can never be terminated; and that
> God's most powerful weapon on earth is a Christian who, when threatened or harmed, refuses to retaliate.

That brings us to the third word in Ephesians 4:2: LONGSUFFERING.

Longsuffering speaks to my attitude toward antagonism.

It's a quality of self-restraint in the face of provocation which does not hastily retaliate or promptly punish.

It's the opposite of anger and is associated with mercy.

It's a trait that's characteristic of God (Exodus 34:6).

It's a trait that is characteristic of Christ (Romans 2:4).

It's a trait that is to characterize my attitude and response to the world (Ephesians 4:2).

It's an attitude that, when learned and practiced, can provide some degree of serenity and a maximum amount of positive influence.

LONGSUFFERING means: I ACCEPT ALL OF MAN'S DEALINGS WITH ME WITHOUT RETALIATION.

It deals with the natural inclination to want to get even.

It deals with my problem of hostility.

It restrains me in the face of opposition.

It displays itself in a gentle answer that turns away wrath (Proverbs 15:1) sometimes. Not always, but sometimes.

In an early pastorate I was confronted by a hostile man who genuinely felt he had some valid grievances against me. He wouldn't list them, however. I confronted him one day in the church building and asked him to tell me how I had offended him. He refused. I stood in the doorway of the furnace room and said, "I am not going to move, my friend, until we can settle this. Will you please tell me what I have done so that I can make it right?"

With that, this incredible hulk of a man grabbed me, lifted me off the floor, and flung me against the opposite wall. I rebounded from that wall, fists clenched, and headed straight for an all-out brawl.

I never did know what happened next. Either I was seeing stars or a brilliant divine display of neon lights. Right before my very eyes were the words, NO STRIKER. In my King James Bible that was listed as one of the qualifications of a pastor. It meant that I could not be a brawler, pugnacious, or a fighter of any kind.

It meant that I could not hit him back.

I stopped in my tracks, unclenched my fists, bowed my head, and walked back to my office without a word.

The Lord was especially kind to me that day. He preserved me from a heap of guilt. He protected me from a brutal beating, and he provided me with a friend for life—for within a few minutes, my world-be enemy was in my office, and together on our knees we were asking forgiveness of each other.

LONGSUFFERING means: I ACCEPT ALL OF MAN'S DEALINGS WITH ME WITHOUT RETALIATION.

Stephen's martyrdom provides the backdrop for illustrating the awesome power of longsuffering. He was the church's first full-fledged martyr—the first member of the new-born church to die for his faith in Christ. After preaching one of history's most convincting sermons, he was stoned. The enraged enemy could not dispose of him quickly enough.

They screamed at him.

They covered their ears as he spoke.

They rushed toward him.

They dragged him out of the city.

They pummelled him with stones until he was not only dead but buried.

His response was: "Lord, do not hold this sin against them!" (Acts 7:60).

One of the agitators who encouraged the murder of Stephen was a man named Saul of Tarsus—later known as the apostle Paul.

This same Saul of Tarsus went from Stephen's murder to ravage the church, going from house to house identifying the early believers and dragging them off to prison. The early Christians were intimidated, imprisoned, martyred, or forced to leave their homes and communities to flee for their lives.

This same Saul intensified his campaign of terror. He broadened his base and moved north from Jerusalem toward Damascus.

It's at this point that the longsuffering of God comes into sharp focus. It's here that we see the infinite patience of Jesus.

The church had just been born.

It was God's baby in this world.

It was small.

It was young.

It was vulnerable, and at the same time it was God's secret weapon.

It was God's hope for earth, and it was supposedly indestructible.

And here was one man—Saul—determined to destroy it, to wipe it clean from the face of the earth. Here was Satan's hit man with his devilish contract already in his pocket, in the process of liquidating the baby church.

If I were God, what would I have done at this point?

Human tendency would have been to defend or retaliate.

Human strategy would have been to eliminate the opposition.

Human inclination would have been to destroy Saul before he destroyed the church.

But not God. He is longsuffering and knows that longsuffering is a far more effective weapon than retaliation.

He waited—and waited—and waited until Saul's vehemence had reached its peak. Then God, in one startling movement, with non-threatening words of love, completely and instantly conquered Saul, broke his heart, captured his spirit, and made him his willing servant for the rest of his life.

Later, Saul of Tarsus wrote letters under the pen name of Paul the apostle. In one addressed to Timothy, his young protégé, he said:

> It is a trustworthy statement, deserving full acceptance, that Christ Jesus came into the world to save sinners, among whom I am foremost of all.
>
> And yet for this reason I found mercy, in order that in me as the foremost, Jesus Christ might demonstrate His perfect patience [longsuffering], as an example for those who would believe in Him for eternal life (1 Timothy 1:15-16).

Paul claims to be the classic illustration of God's longsuffering. If anyone wishes to know how truly patient God is, take a long look at Paul. It was that longsuffering that ultimately claimed Paul as one of God's own.

Jesus' story is even more dramatic than Paul's.

> Jesus resisted death, as is human, but did not reject it.
>
> Jesus felt pain, as is human, but did not plead for mercy.
>
> Jesus cried out to his Father, as is human, but did not scream at his attackers.
>
> Jesus fainted, as is human, but did not renounce his deity.
>
> Jesus was beaten, spat upon, pierced and ridiculed —eventually crucified—but never retaliated— though, unlike others, he could have halted the

entire dying process at any time, had he chosen to do so.

Like Stephen, in place of retaliation he cried: "Father forgive them; for they know not what they are doing" (Luke 23:34).

The end result was the conversion of one of the two criminals hanging nearby. A Roman guard, instrumental in the whole crucifixion process, began praising God and proclaiming Jesus' innocence.

The unbelieving world was awed. The stage was set for a resurrection and the whole world was about to feel the impact of a message of power, a message that proclaims the kind of indestructible life that does not fear death.

Our great fear of death has caused us indestructible ones to weave threads of invisibility about ourselves, retreat into our monastic societies, withdraw into our Christian cultures. This fear has blunted the sharp edge of God's most penetrating and powerful weapon: the life of a fearless believer. Our urges for defense, revenge, or even self-justification have weakened God's tool of long-suffering.

When the recession hit Portland I decided that long-suffering was the only possible weapon that could ease the hostility created by my previous confrontation with the activist community.

We had attacked and we had estranged the very people we were trying to reach.

Longsuffering comes hard for me—and yet if long-suffering can reach a hostile world and at the same time diminish my discomfort level, it deserves maximum attention.

We organized fourteen neighborhood churches into a coalition program for one purpose only: to help the needy. We called it REACH-OUT. It was designed as a pre-evangelism bridge to a hostile neighborhood.

Its genius was in its simplicity.

We recruited volunteers from the local churches with certain skills or interests or those who just had the time and the heart to help needy neighbors.

We advertised our presence and our availability.

We played down any church relationships.

We offered help—with no remuneration, no strings attached.

We went into homes with no verbal witness, simply to meet needs that our neighbors could no longer afford.

We mowed lawns, repaired roofs, shopped for groceries, baby-sat young ones, assisted the elderly, provided medical care, dental care, and home nursing, repaired automobiles, moved furniture, repaired plumbing, and offered transportation.

We fed, we clothed, and we housed needy neighbors.

In two years the church, by invitation, moved into 1800 neighborhood homes. Ninety-five percent of these were unchurched families. Since that time, the feelings of hostility have eased. Many have come to Christ.

One family of Vietnamese refugees established a restaurant across the street from the church. We patronized their establishment, helped them financially, and even housed and clothed them when their building was destroyed by fire. They all received Christ. Before leaving the community the mother came to me and said, "For years people have been telling me to find Christ. I did not know where to look for him. When you and your people came to me to help me, I knew that finally I had found him and now I have grown to love him."

Longsuffering is not just a term of response—it is a term that denotes action. It initiates action. It moves toward the hostile and the frightening with overtures of love and caring.

I am learning longsuffering, not only toward a hostile world, but also toward some forms of hostility that I have found in my own world—and it works.

It is freeing me.

Longsuffering draws beauty out of ugliness. It replaces fear with love and causes one to have a dynamic influence upon the very people whom it once feared.

I learned an interesting fact about my giant silk moth—the silk moth that still hasn't emerged from its ugly cocoon. The moth that remains hidden within its own web will have but one purpose when it emerges. During its life expectancy of ten days or less, its sole purpose will be to reproduce.

It will have no interest in its own comfort or its own longevity. It will only concentrate on one thing—to reproduce itself.

My purpose is similar. I'm here to reproduce people of like kind, of like faith.

This can never be accomplished from within the confines of a cocoon. This will never be achieved in isolation. It can never be accomplished if I withdraw into hiding.

Longsuffering accepts all that man does to me without retaliation, a definition which presupposes risks, which demands vulnerability, and which means I willingly move out of the trenches into the front lines. With my face to those who would oppose me, I readily display the power and majesty of a patient God through the medium of a serene, non-threatened, and indestructible life.

"The ultimate act of divine strategy is to take unbelieving, alienated, lonely, diverse, hostile humanity and make them into friends."

Chapter Twelve

Accepting . . . Our Differences

LOWLINESS OF MIND says

I ACCEPT ALL THAT GOD SAYS ABOUT ME WITHOUT ARGUMENT—and enables me to accept myself.

MEEKNESS says

I ACCEPT ALL OF GOD'S DEALINGS WITH ME WITHOUT RESISTANCE OR BITTER-NESS—and enables me to accept my God.

LONGSUFFERING says

I ACCEPT ALL OF MAN'S DEALINGS WITH ME WITHOUT RETALIATION—and enables me to accept my enemies.

FORBEARANCE says

I ACCEPT YOU WITH ALL OF YOUR FAULTS OR OUR DIFFERENCES—and enables me to accept even my friends.

A Chinese man and a Jewish man were having dinner together. During their conversation the Jewish man suddenly became silent. A look of hostility spread over his face. Without a word he doubled his fist, drew back his arm, swung, and hit the Chinese man full in the side of the head.

The Chinese man toppled from his chair, sprawled on the floor and lay still. After a few moments he lifted himself slightly, shook his head, looked at his friend, and said, "Why in the world did you do that?"

The Jewish man answered, "That's for Pearl Harbor!"

"Pearl Harbor?" the Chinese man asked. "Friend," he said, "the Chinese had nothing to do with Pearl Harbor. It was the Japanese air force that bombed Pearl Harbor."

The Chinese man climbed back into his chair and resumed his dinner.

Suddenly a look of hostility spread across his face, and he, without a word, doubled his fist, drew back his arm, swung with all his might, and struck the Jewish man in the side of his head.

The Jewish man toppled from his chair, sprawled on the floor, and lay silent for a moment. He then lifted himself from the floor, shook his head and asked, "Why in the world did you do that?"

"That was for the Titanic!" the Chinese man answered.

"The Titanic?" the Jewish man exclaimed. "The Jews didn't sink the Titanic, that was an iceberg."

"An iceberg," exclaimed the Chinese man, "well—Goldberg, Feinberg, Iceberg—what's the difference?"

The story, of course, is apocryphal, but the lesson is easily applied.

It's a rare conflict of any kind in which anyone is fully aware of the issues involved and an even rarer conflict in which one side holds all the moral turf.

Whether we're considering the war between Iran and Iraq; the never-ending struggle in Beirut between the Druse, Moslems, and the Phalangists; the Irish hostility between Catholics and Protestants; the struggle between the leftist guerrillas and the Sandinista regime in Nicaragua; the Sikhs and the Hindus; the Zulu struggle with their class warfare; the political conflicts between Democrats and Republicans; the theological struggles between Evangelicals and Fundamentalists; the sexist battles between men and women; the racist wars between blacks and whites; the marital turmoil between husband and wife; or the family squabbles between parent and child, the questions of why we are fighting and who is responsible are not always clear.

There are countless soldiers and civilians who have died for causes that were no more clearly defined than those battles between people who butter their bread right side up and those who butter their bread upside down.

Forbearance is in desperately short supply in today's human race—and especially rare in the church of Jesus Christ.

I have watched various local churches and denominations and Christian organizations with bewilderment as they have allowed one crisis after another to sap them of their strength and separate them.

Since I've been a Baptist most of my life, I can tell this story. A speaker was tracing the origin of Baptists. "Many of you trace the history of Baptists back to the sixteenth century," he said. "Some of you trace their beginnings back to the second chapter of the Book of Acts—others to John the Baptist. I think you're all wrong," he said. "I think the Baptist church was founded in Genesis, chapter 13, where Abraham said to Lot, "You go your way, and I'll go mine."

No church in history had greater potential for division than the early New Testament church.

Racial, cultural, ethnic, social, philosophical, and even theological issues were so diverse that any form of union seemed totally impossible.

But God performed the ultimate act of divine strategy on an unbelieving, alienated, hostile, lonely, diverse humanity.

He took the two most antagonistic, impossibly

different races of people—the Jews with their long history of traditional religion and the Gentiles with their long history of pagan polytheism. Bringing these two groups together, he broke down "irreconcilable differences," melted their hearts toward each other, wound their arms about each other's bodies, and caused them to plant loving, holy kisses on each other's cheeks.

He made them bow together, pray together, weep together, sing together, share together, preach together, and even die together. The first great miracle after Christ's resurrection was the merging of two totally diverse peoples into one body of believing Christians. The impact of this miracle was so great that the unbelieving world stood back in awe and watched with wonder.

God intended that act to be an ongoing miracle—an ever-present source of wonder. Paul exhorts us in Ephesians 4:3 to be "diligent to preserve the unity of the Spirit . . ."

I doubt that there has been a time in church history when there has been so much diversity of thinking, so much potential difference of opinion, so much opportunity for downright division.

The world of Christians, just like the world of non-Christians, has polarized around so many sensitive issues that it would seem unity or oneness could easily become an elusive dream.

The church has become very political—that's not bad unless it allows politics to divide it.

In 1976 my intense interest in the political campaign was heightened by the fact that the Oregon campaign manager for the Republican presidential nominee was an active member of Hinson Church. The treasurer for the Democratic presidential nominee was also an active member of the Hinson family. These two men and their families were close friends and fellow-Christians.

I watched with great interest and prayed with much fervor for them both. As the campaign increased in its intensity, I marveled at the manner in which these men dealt with their differences. The world was so amazed a this phenomenon it was recorded in a local newspaper.

Is spiritual unity a real life option where there is so much diversity?

Spiritual unity is not the absence of differences—spiritual unity is the absence of division.

Spiritual unity is the merging of humans from different ethnic backgrounds, different social, economic, and cultural experiences, different theological and religious orientations—people of different colors, sizes, and shapes—into one unique Spiritual Body.

The individual never loses his uniqueness or his distinctiveness. He never loses his identity. He does surrender, however, his intolerance toward specific people and ideas.

That brings us to the fourth word in Ephesians 4:2: FORBEARANCE.

> Forbearance means to "hold up,"
>   "to bear with equanimity,"
>   "to sustain,"
>   "to endure with patience,"
>   "to be tolerant."
> It addresses the problems of bigotry and bias.
> It speaks to any form of chauvinism or feminism.
> It breaks down all the real or imagined barriers
>   that separate people.

FORBEARANCE means:
I ACCEPT YOU IN SPITE OF YOUR FAULTS OR OUR DIFFERENCES.

Forbearance solves the very real and very human problems of loneliness and alienation.

It means that I am accepted in spite of what is unacceptable about me.

I am welcomed in spite of what I think.

I am received in spite of how I look.

I am encouraged even in spite of what I believe.

Forbearance accepts, in spite of what it knows.

There's a little song sung by Australian children that goes:

> The perfect friend is one who knows the worst
>   about you
> and loves you just the same.
> There's only one who loves like that, and Jesus is
>   his name.

Romans 14:1 commands forbearance: "Now accept the one who is weak in faith, but not for the purpose of passing judgment on his opinions."

The Scriptures plead for high levels of tolerance in such diverse areas as what we eat or what we drink or even when and where we worship. It requires conformity only where the doctrine of Christ is at stake, the plan of salvation is at issue, or where Christian morality is being abused.

I must admit right here to some problems. I'm breaking free—but it's a painful process.

I have been plagued with a somewhat restrained Archie Bunker mentality—a mindset that tolerated more bigotry than it should have. I'm still tempted, at times, to laugh at ethnic jokes. I am still conscious of racial backgrounds and cultural differences.

I still struggle with thoughts of male chauvinism—but God is giving me a new heart in recent days. I'm overwhelmed when I stop to think about it—it's almost too much to write about.

It's a heart that has begun to beat with a compassion for the hurting, a new sensitivity for the fallen, a greater understanding for the weak. It's a heart that seems to be enlarging itself to embrace those unloved, unwanted, unaccepted ones who have been made lonely by the alienation of a judgmental church.

It's a heart that no longer repels or rejects.

It's a heart that has finally come to realize that the power of acceptance is the greatest life-changing force in all the world.

It's a heart that has finally caught the great truth of Scripture that teaches that *love never commands obedience— love produces obedience.*

In Luke, chapter 19, we see a classic illustration of what forbearance will do in a life. Do you remember Zacchaeus? He was that little Jewish rebel who alienated himself from all his friends and neighbors by selling out to the Roman government. He became a chief tax collector—which means he made himself rich by taxing Jews and then gouging them above what they really owed in order to line his own pockets. Zacchaeus, along with other tax collectors, was among the most hated of all Jewish citizens. He was regarded with contempt, he was alienated, he was friendless, he was empty, alone, hostile. An outcast.

When Jesus arrived in Zacchaeus' home town of Jericho, however, the diminutive IRS man was curious— so curious that he climbed into a sycamore tree for a better look at the Savior.

When Jesus came to the place, without warning and without any apparent reason he looked up and began to address Zacchaeus.

It was right here in Jericho, beneath a sycamore tree, in the presence of the city's biggest cheat, that Jesus displayed forbearance. With complete acceptance he looked at Zacchaeus and said, "Zacchaeus, hurry, come down, for today I must stay at your house." Zacchaeus heard it, came down, and received Jesus gladly.

Can you imagine the reaction of the crowd? The Scriptures say they grumbled and criticized Jesus for being the guest of a sinner.

As Jesus and Zacchaeus walked toward that house, something big, something wonderful, happened in that little man's heart. Zacchaeus stopped and said, "Behold, Lord (notice how he called him Lord—something had already happened to convince Zacchaeus that he was in the presence of God), half of my possessions I will give to the poor, and if I've defrauded anyone of anything, I will give back four times as much" (Luke 19:8).

What had happened? Had Jesus preached on stealing—demanded repentance—commanded restoration? No. The accepting, forgiving spirit of Jesus unlocked within Zacchaeus the ability to respond to God.

Jesus accepted him, in spite of his faults, and as a result was able to change him.

The most amazing example of forbearance to me, however, is not Zacchaeus, or others like Judas or Matthew or Thomas or Peter or the Samaritan or the thief on the cross. All of these are overshadowed by Jesus' acceptance of me.

The older I get, the more I am made aware of my sin. It seems that my wicked heart never improves, my flesh never weakens, my carnal nature never subsides. The longer I live, the more I marvel at the forbearance of God—forbearance that accepts me in spite of my faults and loves me in spite of my sin.

I often have opportunity to display forbearance when engaging in various forms of church discipline. My first act when moving in to begin restoring a fallen brother is to take him in my arms and hold him close and long, simply to reassure him that I accept him in spite of his faults.

This single act has done more to ease and to hasten the restoration process than any other thing that I could say or do.

Forbearance is on display every Sunday at Hinson Church. Located in an activist, low-income neighborhood, this cosmopolitan congregation constantly welcomes the poor, the lame, the retarded, the hostile, the old, the young. I'm terribly proud of their forbearance.

One Sunday Bruce Wilkinson of "Walk Thru the Bible" was presenting a dramatic portrayal of the book of Habakkuk. The players were costumed. All attention was directed to the platform when suddenly and quietly one of the student actors slipped through the doors in the back of the auditorium in preparation for a dramatic down-the-aisle entrance.

He was dressed like a Chaldean soldier in a toga, leggings, beard, and headpiece—which was not too different from some of the far-out dress we saw daily in our neighborhood.

I watched as one of our senior members turned around from his place in the back row. He spotted this strange creature—gave him a startled look—sat there for a few moments in bewilderment and then stood up and walked toward him.

I was certain that he was going to ask him to leave.

Instead, he walked over to the young man, smiled and asked him if he would like to have his seat. In doing so he almost spoiled a dramatic moment, but the action spoke volumes: Hinson was learning forbearance.

Forbearance says, I ACCEPT YOU IN SPITE OF YOUR FAULTS OR OUR DIFFERENCES.

> Forbearance produces unified churches.
> Forbearance creates harmonious marriages.
> Forbearance develops happy families.
> Forbearance, like longsuffering, is the church's evangelistic weapon. It totally disarms the alienated, overwhelming them with a feeling of love that's irresistible.
> Forbearance is the result of getting to know each other.

Hinson has established growth groups, supportive fellowships, and all sorts of small group activities for the purpose of getting acquainted. It's impossible to fully love someone we don't know—to understand and trust someone who is a stranger to us.

William was in his late twenties, a resident of mental institutions and foster homes all his life. When the recession hit Oregon, he was of the many placed in neighborhood homes near the church. He dressed like a character out of Doonesbury—coonskin cap, dark glasses, heavy leather jacket, and high boots. He always came late to church and always walked across the front of the auditorium to sit right below the pulpit.

Every time I gave an invitation, he was the first to come forward. After it had happened so many times I sensed the people fidget and heard their subdued snickers. It began to pose such a problem that people refused to come forward, and I almost stopped extending invitations.

No matter how many times we talked to him, he continued to come.

One Sunday evening he came again. The congregation watched him with disgust.

As we paused in our singing, I walked over to him and asked him publicly, "William, why is it you like to come forward every time we close the service?"

He took the microphone from my hand and said, "Pastor, it's because I know you love me, and I just like to come and stand beside you."

From that moment, that bit of knowledge made him not only acceptable but loved by all the people.

To accept you—I must get to know you.

Forbearance is beautiful—irresistibly beautiful. When visible, it catches the eye of the admirer and holds the attention of the beholder.

Forbearance is the freedom to accept as I have been accepted. It's the awesome joy of performing the unexpected act that causes cocoons to fall away and beautiful creatures to emergy.

> It erases hostility.
> It eliminates alienation.
> It dispels loneliness.

Forbearance can make caterpillars feel accepted—even though they haven't yet emerged—even though they haven't shed their binding webs—even though they haven't been transformed.

In fact, it's this kind of acceptance that *enables* caterpillars to emerge. It's the kind of acceptance that creates butterflies, giving wings to those encased by their own bondage.

"To continue to feel
comfortable with
ourselves and others
requires periodic
maintenance. Even right
relationships can
go wrong."

Chapter Thirteen

Maintenance and Repair

Even right relationships can go wrong at times. As I have learned to live comfortably with myself, I still find times of self-doubt when reassurance is needed. I still find that those neurotic little notions creep in and stir some of the old anxieties to life.

When doubts about my relationship with God through Christ emerge, I go to the Scriptures. I let God reassure me from his own Word.

When uncomfortable feelings about one of my friends begin to float through my consciousness—feelings that seem to have no basis in fact—I go to my friend. I let him listen, and as he listens, I listen to myself. What is my subconscious trying to say? Simply verbalizing those feelings usually helps me to sort out what's real from what is only imagined.

When relationships with a brother are disturbed through anger or misunderstanding, I go to my brother.

I served on the staff at Hinson from 1957 to 1960 as an associate pastor. I left that position with ill-feeling toward a deacon who had been a dear friend. Fourteen years later I returned to Hinson as senior pastor. On my first Sunday I went to find him—before I preached. I took him aside, asked forgiveness for my offense, received it, and was free to preach.

Another friend, an officer of a different church, and I broke fellowship over a difference of opinion. For years that was the strongest lingering memory of that seven-year ministry. Every time I thought of that church, Bob's face would come into focus, and I would grieve over that unhappy memory.

He came to Hinson one Sunday night years later. It was communion Sunday. As we gathered for an evening around the Lord's Table, I spotted him, halfway back, center section, and our eyes met.

I proceeded to teach, briefly, and then as I lifted the bread plate to pass it to my deacons, I was forced to stop. I put the plate down and said, "I'm sorry, I can't go on. There's a brother here in this audience whom I offended nearly twelve years ago. I have never asked his forgiveness. He knows who I'm talking about—no one else needs to." I asked the audience to all bow their heads and pray. I looked straight at him, and he looked straight at me, and I said, "My brother, will you forgive me?" A broad smile crossed his face, his head bobbed up and down, and I was free.

After the service he came to me, threw his arms about me and said, "You know—if you hadn't done that tonight, I think I would have. I knew it had to be settled tonight."

To feel comfortable with ourselves and with others requires periodic maintenance. Even right relationships can go wrong.

That delightful relationship we have with God cannot be disturbed, but its enjoyment can certainly be diminished. When I feel uncomfortable with God, it's never his fault. It's always mine, and I go to him. I acknowledge the sin that has disturbed our fellowship, claim his forgiveness, and carry on.

When the world threatens me, I go to my knees as Jesus did in the Garden of Gethsemane. That's the only place where courage and strength can be secured to meet the threats of a hostile world that's determined to destroy me, just as it did Jesus.

To continue to feel comfortable in all of life's relationships demands constant awareness and sometimes minor or major repair. But whatever it takes, it requires immediate attention and is always worth the effort.

_____

"My butterfly broke free
this morning."

_____

Chapter Fourteen

Out of Hiding

My butterfly broke free this morning. It shed its trappings, slipped out of its bindings, worked its way out of its web of silk, and left its prison house behind. The cocoon is finally empty, the butterfly is finally free.

The final act of freedom really didn't take long. It was so fast I almost missed it. Quite suddenly I detected a little movement on the tip of the cocoon next to the twig. An ugly worm-like creature began to appear. It struggled as it fought its way out of its bondage until, suddenly free at last, it spread those two magnificent wings and revealed itself as a new creation in all of its extraordinary beauty.

You may question my credibility at this point, but let me assure you—as incidental as it may seem to you—that when I couldn't get started writing this book, the cocoon arrived, and as I'm finishing this last chapter, the butterfly appeared.

It's absolutely beautiful. Technically, of course, it's not a butterfly at all, but a giant silk moth—larger than any I've ever seen. Its wing span exceeds six inches. Its body is the thickness and length of a large peanut—but far more colorful. The long, feathery antennae tell me it's a boy.

The symmetrical markings on its wing and the wide range of colors are stunning. The broad, strong wings are a deep green, ringed with reds and whites, with tips that are almost transparent. Its body is striped red and white. Its head and legs are a deep red. Each dark green wing has a perfectly shaped quarter-moon design in white, right in the center.

What a contrast to the ugly, dull, boring brown which housed it for so long. What a delight to see life, energy, and movement in place of the lifelessness of that cocoon.

And it flies! From the moment of its transformation it has pumped its magnificent wings open and closed in preparation for its flight to complete freedom.

I experienced some similar sensations when I broke free from my deep depression years ago. I have enjoyed repeated experiences of this freeing process each time I've gained some new insight into myself, some new truth about God, some new understanding of others.

And each time I dwell on any or all of these simple, life-changing words and then find opportunity to employ them, I experience a new degree of freedom—actually feel a new freedom.

Notice these four words or phrases one more time:

LOWLINESS OF MIND:

> *I accept all that God says about me without argument.*
> To accept myself, I get to know the Scriptures.
> To feel accepted, I employ "thank you therapy," the simple act of offering repeated thank you's to God for what is true about me, whether it feels true or not.

MEEKNESS:

> *I accept all of God's dealings with me without resistance or bitterness.*

In order to accept all of life's circumstances, I accept the truths about God—all of them—and again employ "thank you therapy," giving thanks in everything. Believing that everything has been allowed by a sovereign, loving, heavenly Father—whether I like it or not.

LONGSUFFERING:

I accept all of man's dealings with me without retaliation.
To feel accepted or comfortable in a hostile world, I thank God for my indestructibility as an eternal person. I also thank him for the privilege of touching lives with a response that will ultimately bring about change.

FORBEARANCE:

I accept you with all your faults or our differences.
In order to accept another person or feel accepted by another person, I must get to know that person. I must then thank God for him, and even for the differences that will stretch my tolerance and love levels to their limit.

The process in my own life is far from complete. I still find some of the debris from that old cocoon hanging on to me from time to time. At other times I actively resist these truths, and am tempted to go back into hiding.

As I was concluding this chapter, Martha and I were located on the top floor of the Prince Kuhio Hotel near Waikiki Beach in Hawaii, in the middle of a badly needed vacation.

We retired early Saturday evening. The last thing we talked about was which morning worship service we would attend Sunday morning—the early service or the later one.

I said, "You know, I'm so tired, I may not go to church at all in the morning."

We were awakened at 6:30 with the news that the pastor of the church we were going to attend had become suddenly and seriously ill. I was asked to preach both ser-vices in his place.

As we were driving to the church, I turned to Martha and said, "I'm sorry, but right now I don't feel the least bit meek, nor do I wish to. I really wanted to rest this morn-ing."

As soon as I had unleashed those feelings, we were able to thank God for an unexpected and unplanned ex-perience and believe that a sovereign God had rear-ranged our day for reasons known only to him.

To come out of hiding, to open myself up to myself and to my God and to others, has been a wonderfully freeing experience.

I covet it for you.

Remember:

> In order to feel comfortable with myself—I must get to know myself as God reveals me in the Scrip-tures.

> In order to feel comfortable with God, I must get to know God as he reveals himself in the Scrip-tures.

> In order to feel comfortable in a hostile world, I must get to know Jesus, and he is revealed as the truly longsuffering One in the Scriptures.

> In order to feel comfortable with you, I must get to know you as you slowly (and perhaps fearfully) reveal yourself to me.

And then, in the experience of spiritual unity and peace, we can display the magnificent beauty that is char-acteristic of the body of Christ, we can pollinate the world with the wonder of Jesus and see our own serene, com-fortable, acceptable selves reproduced in the lives of others still struggling to become free.

True acceptance, however, must have a starting point. It can begin at only one place, and that is at the cross of Jesus Christ.

It's there that I acknowledge my bondage to sin, and it is there I admit that the only liberating force in the world is Jesus Christ.

It is there that I confess my helplessness, reach out for his love and grace, and experience the power of his forgiveness.

It is there that the limitless power of God is unleashed in my life . . . a power that makes a life of acceptance possible . . . a power that enables me to reach out in every direction . . . a power that allows me to be comfortable in a most uncomfortable world.